SPYING, SURVEILLANCE, AND
PRIVACY IN THE 21st CENTURY

21st-Century Surveillance Technologies

Daniel E. Harmon

Cavendish
Square

New York

Published in 2018 by Cavendish Square Publishing, LLC
243 5th Avenue, Suite 136, New York, NY 10016

Copyright © 2018 by Cavendish Square Publishing, LLC

First Edition

Library of Congress Cataloging-in-Publication Data

Names: Harmon, Daniel E.
Title: 21st-century surveillance technologies / Daniel E. Harmon.
Description: New York : Cavendish Square, 2018. | Series: Spying, surveillance, and privacy in the 21st-century | Includes index.
Identifiers: ISBN 9781502626745 (library bound) | ISBN 9781502626691 (ebook)
Subjects: LCSH: Electronic surveillance--Juvenile literature.
| Security systems--Juvenile literature.
Classification: LCC TK7882.E2 H37 2018 | DDC 005.8--dc23

Editorial Director: David McNamara
Editor: Fletcher Doyle
Copy Editor: Nathan Heidelberger
Associate Art Director: Amy Greenan
Designer: Stephanie Flecha
Production Coordinator: Karol Szymczuk
Photo Research: J8 Media

The photographs in this book are used by permission and through the courtesy of:
Cover Erik Simonsen/Photographer's Choice/Getty Images; p. 6 Gregory R Todd, rotated by Artem Korzhimanov/Wikimedia Commons/File:Dawn of the Space Age (rotated).jpg/CC BY SA 3.0; p. 7 Bride Lane Library/Popperfoto/Getty Images; p. 11 Franck Reporter/E+/Getty Images; p. 17 NSA/Wikimedia Commons/File:National Security Agency headquarters, Fort Meade, Maryland.jpg/Public Domain; p. 19 Corbis/Getty Images; p. 23 Naoto Anazawa/U.S. Air Force/Wikimedia Commons/File:Traffic control (15961154490).jpg/Public Domain; p. 26 NASA; p. 39 PA Images/Alamy Stock Photo; p. 41 Matthew J. Lee/The Boston Globe/Getty Images; p. 43 catnap72/E+/Getty Images; p. 45 Money Sharma/AFP/Getty Images; p. 49 FBI; p. 52 Etaphop photo/Shutterstock.com; p. 56 Tarso Sarraf/picture-alliance/dpa/AP Images; p. 62 Bertrand Langlois/AFP/Getty Images; p. 66 Kathy deWitt/Alamy Stock Photo; p. 70 Andre Kudyusov/Photodisc/Getty Images; p. 75 Jinxy Productions/Blend Images/Getty Images; p. 78 By Kletr/Shutterstock.com; p. 82 Trevor Chriss/Alamy Stock Photo; p. 85 Thomas Monaster/NY Daily News Archive/Getty Images; p. 87 Andrew Cribb/Alamy Stock Photo; p. 89 Larry Ellis/Express/Getty Images.
Printed in the United States of America

Contents

An artist's rendering shows *Sputnik* in orbit around Earth. *Sputnik I* was launched in October 1957.

CHAPTER 1

A New Age in Surveillance Technology

The world entered a startling, uncertain new era on October 4, 1957. TASS, the Russian news agency, issued a sensational report that the Soviet Union had successfully launched the world's first man-made satellite, *Sputnik I*, into orbit around Earth. The craft took only an hour and a half to complete a circuit around the globe.

It was the time of the Cold War. During World War II (1939–1945), Germany, the United States, and the Soviet Union began developing nuclear weapons programs. After the war ended, the two emerging superpowers accelerated rocket and missile testing, each seeking to gain an advantage over the other. By the time the first *Sputnik* was launched, an attitude of gloom had spread worldwide. World War III, doomsayers warned, would end the human race. Until the breakup of the Soviet Union in the late 1980s and early 1990s, international politics and economic strategies were affected by Cold War jockeying for nuclear and military supremacy.

As Americans pondered the implications of *Sputnik*, they became unnerved. Thousands ventured out uneasily at night to scrutinize the sky, looking for the tiny bright speck moving across the starry tapestry in its periodic transit. A thought ran through the minds of millions: The Russians are taking aerial photographs of our military installations. Satellite cameras even could be photographing us as we walk our streets and relax in our yards.

The fear would prove to be greatly exaggerated—but not entirely baseless. The United States launched its own first satellite only three months later. These early Soviet and American satellites mainly were engineered not to take pictures but to record scientific data concerning the upper atmosphere, such as its temperature, density, and chemical composition. Soon enough, though, dedicated spy satellites became a reality.

The military spy programs of many countries besides the United States and Russia have benefited greatly from space technology. The rate of advance has been astonishing. However, the extraordinary capability of state-of-the-art, high-altitude **reconnaissance** instruments is but one facet of twenty-first-century surveillance technology. Government agencies, police departments, detective services, criminal organizations, and ordinary individuals now have remarkable snooping tools at their disposal that were undreamed of when the first *Sputnik* went into orbit.

This has presented a problem. The astonishing capabilities of surveillance technology in the twenty-first century have enabled scientists, peacekeepers, and emergency responders to understand, foresee, and react to a world of global crises and neighborhood emergencies. At the same time, they have triggered suspicions of privacy invasion—which in fact occurs, in one form or another, every day.

The Pinkerton eye illustrated the dectective agency's main investigative tool: visual surveillance.

The famous Pinkerton National Detective Agency, founded in 1850, adopted as its motto the stern warning phrase "We Never Sleep." The implication was that its growing staff of detectives was at work around the clock to bring criminals to justice. Today, in the same vein, surveillance never stops. Powered by more and more sophisticated technology, many types of surveillance occur worldwide from the air and the sea, as well as on land. Surveillance also pervades the internet.

Whenever you enter a public place—school grounds, a city sidewalk, a mall, a supermarket, a restaurant, a park, a passenger plane—you may be losing control over your privacy.

Cyber Surveillance in Politics

One or more **hackers** gained access to email memos that were transmitted among staff members of the Democratic National Committee (DNC) during the 2016 presidential election campaign. In July of that year—just days before the Democratic National Convention began—almost twenty thousand of the messages were released by WikiLeaks. They contained controversial exchanges in which, for example, Democratic political operatives had discussed ways to disparage Senator Bernie Sanders of Vermont, the leading party rival to Hillary Clinton during the primary season. As a result of the email scandal, DNC Chairwoman Debbie Wasserman Schultz and other committee leaders were forced to resign.

WikiLeaks, which began operations in 2006, is an international nonprofit organization famous—some would say infamous—for publishing leaked **classified** information that has embarrassed governments, political figures and factions, and businesses. Many believe it has jeopardized security in certain regions. Its hacker sources are anonymous, as are most of its leaders. Julian Assange, an Australian, is the founder and publisher.

According to its mission statement posted at www.wikileaks.org, "WikiLeaks specializes in the analysis and publication of large datasets of censored or otherwise restricted official materials involving war, spying and corruption." As of late 2016, it claimed to have published more than ten million documents and related material.

The US State Department ordered an investigation of the DNC scandal to determine who had infiltrated the committee's email servers, and why. US officials cast heavy suspicion on Russian operatives, possibly sponsored by the Russian government. The assumed reason was that the Russians were opposed to Clinton's presidential candidacy. Russia's leaders denied involvement.

Many people suspected Russia of interfering with America's electoral process. Most Democrats naturally were infuriated and called for federal security and law enforcement agencies to trace the source of the leaks. Some Republicans, although they may have been generally leery of WikiLeaks, countered that American voters had a right to know about the DNC's inside maneuverings, which were exposed. They also denied there was proof of Russian involvement.

Regardless, the episode raised serious concerns about the use of cyber technology internationally. Spying between countries and political rivals has been a fact of life for thousands of years. Political tampering by foreign governments is not unheard of. However, the ubiquitous internet, a platform used by legions of **cybercriminals**, has focused the attention of privacy advocates more intently on the realm of cyber surveillance.

Someone unnoticed could be taking your picture or recording a video or sound clip of you. A stranger passing by could be wearing a video camera pen, recording unflattering remarks you're making to a companion. In the twenty-first century, it's conceivable that you're caught on "candid camera" every day. Your image and voice could turn up on social media platforms in a very embarrassing light.

Surveillance from Every Vantage Point

Extraordinary advances in technology, particularly during the last half century, have impacted the practice of surveillance dramatically. New inventions and constantly improving systems are providing more sophisticated capabilities almost daily. Methods of observation and monitoring that were unheard of in the 1950s are resulting in beneficial—and sometimes troubling—actions.

Visual and audio recording equipment is in constant operation above and around us. Also, monitoring of electronic devices is contributing to a growing realm of data collection and analysis about individuals and their habits.

View from the Air

Aerial surveillance is conducted from a variety of positions, ranging from several feet above the ground to several hundred miles in space. Satellites and high-flying spy planes can record photographs and videos of earthly activities, including the movements of humans, in remarkable detail. Closer to the ground, unpiloted aerial vehicles (UAVs), or drones, are used by military branches and police agencies. They also are used by ordinary people. Some fly them for fun. Others fly them with devious intentions.

Police helicopters provide aerial views of crime and disaster scenes, as well as traffic conditions.

The United States began developing reconnaissance satellites in 1955. By the end of that decade, they were in orbit. Every US president since then, Democrat and Republican, has acknowledged the benefits of using reconnaissance spacecraft technology for national security and humanitarian purposes. Critics point out that while executing their laudable missions, they also are gathering data that might compromise individuals' privacy.

To begin orbiting Earth, a space satellite must be launched to an altitude of at least 120 miles (200 kilometers) above Earth's surface. To avoid being pulled back by gravity, it must move extremely fast—at least 18,000 miles per hour (29,000 kilometers per hour). Some large satellites can be seen at night, moving almost imperceptibly across the starry sky. In fact, they are zooming through space at a blistering rate.

Within Earth's atmosphere, surveillance regularly is conducted by military airplanes around the world. Closer to the ground, helicopters equipped with the latest technology are used by emergency responders, including medical facilities and police, as well as by military units.

Piloted planes and helicopters are not the only surveillance craft in the lower atmosphere. Increasingly, different branches of the military as well as federal, state, county, and municipal law enforcement agencies are using drones. Surveillance is the most common type of mission. Purposes are as routine as daily rush hour traffic monitoring and as dramatic as documenting active crime and disaster scenes and the movements of military antagonists. Special operations units in the military also have used drones to remotely control electronic assets and to launch weapons.

Drones are among the modern technology tools deployed by US Border Patrol agents. A single UAV camera reportedly can scan activity within a range of several miles, alerting officers on the ground to respond. These drones can set up a virtual fence along a border, and no one except the agents will know it is there.

Besides military units and police departments, private detectives use drones to obtain evidence. Their clients include insurance companies that suspect fraud on the part of customers who claim false personal injuries or property damage, or who exaggerate medical conditions. Clients also include parties involved in lawsuits, particularly in divorce and **child custody** battles. Investigators who work for law firms use drones for basically the same purposes.

Hobbyists, including children, are buying drones that have notable surveillance powers. An effective low-altitude drone fitted with a high-quality video camera can be bought at department stores or from online retailers for less than $100. These inexpensive UAVs generally are considered toys—but surveillance professionals as well as hobbyists have deployed them effectively.

Land Surveillance

Millions of surveillance cameras, some of them cleverly concealed or disguised, constantly monitor the activities of individuals and vehicles. They are installed indoors and outdoors at public sites, business locations, grade schools and colleges, airports, various government institutions, private residences, and even in large churches. Electronic surveillance commonly is used by local, state, and federal law enforcement agencies. It also is an important tool for security companies and private detective agencies.

In some locations, two or more aerial surveillance cameras are installed in "nests," with the combined lenses covering every direction. Vans and delivery trucks parked on the street for extended periods may be law enforcement or private detective platforms equipped with remote-controlled cameras and microphones.

Thousands of business and industry sites are equipped with security monitoring cameras. Typically, they are installed in elevated locations, some of them hidden, others in clear view from below. They serve two purposes: to record suspicious actions committed by visitors and to record suspicious actions committed by a company's own employees, agents, and contractors. The fulfillment centers of major online retail sellers have scores of ceiling video cameras installed throughout each massive building. The cameras constantly monitor employee activities in every nook and cranny, from different angles. The purpose is to deter employees from stealing from the shelves.

Many other types of businesses are video-recording their employees at work. They do this not just to detect illicit activities but to monitor and evaluate job performance.

A type of electronic surveillance technology still used regularly after more than a century is telephone eavesdropping, commonly known as **wiretapping**. The telephone came into common use beginning in the 1890s, and telephone surveillance by police soon followed. Telephone surveillance has been utilized by the government agencies overseen by every US president since that time. It also is used by state and local law enforcement agencies. At the same time, it has been used by criminals.

Sea Surveillance

Surveillance technology regularly is used by naval ships and associated aircraft. Commanders use it to protect their vessels and **flotillas**. Surveillance technology also is used for government spying from ships and seaplanes. Governments have also tapped into undersea communications cables to monitor international telephone conversations.

In civilian waters, surveillance tech has become essential in the work of monitoring the movements of marine fish and mammals and of water police craft on patrol. Unfortunately, some of the same technology is deployed by twenty-first-century pirates and smugglers in areas such as the Caribbean and the Pacific Rim.

Virtual Surveillance

Federal, state, county, and city governments have been collecting information about citizens since the early years

Deep and Dark

To internet technologists, "Onionland" is one of the terms given to the **deep web**. The so-called deep web is the section of the internet's World Wide Web that most casual browsers never enter. Interestingly, it is by far the largest segment.

The deep web is used by legitimate researchers in quest of obscure information not readily discoverable using Google, Firefox, or other popular search platforms. Museum archivists use it. Lawyers and legal librarians use it. But the deep web also is used by searchers who don't want anyone to know who they are or what they are searching for.

While the deep web generally is a valid resource for everyone, there also is what's called the dark web. There, criminals upload and offer for sale stolen data about millions of individuals. The dark web provides anonymity. If bank account numbers and other customer details are hacked from a major retailer's online database, that information may be for sale on the dark web.

You may be there: your full name, residential address, phone number, email and social media addresses, date and place of birth; details about your parents and siblings; your social security and driver's license numbers; your mother's maiden name; your school records; your interests; photographs of you and your relatives and friends.

People with devious intentions can learn a lot about almost anyone if they know how to use the dark web. The dark web and its vast contents exemplify what can go wrong with surveillance technology in the twenty-first century.

of America's history. This information includes census, tax, property, and criminal records. Beginning in the twentieth century, more and more data were computerized. Today, workers in numerous government offices can turn up myriad details about any citizen with a quick computer records search.

Financial institutions, meanwhile, gather data about everyone with whom they conduct transactions. Information includes bank accounts, loans, credit cards, etc. Like government records, almost all of this information now is digital. It can be searched and analyzed quickly with computers.

The advent of powerful, easy-to-use computers in the 1980s inspired millions of small businesses, professional practices, and individuals to begin maintaining data concerning their customers, clients, and personal contacts. They use the information for quick reference and as a means to provide better service. Businesses also analyze the information for marketing purposes. This is a form of data surveillance in which they keep track of customers' and clients' interests and buying habits.

Who Uses Surveillance Technology?

Modern technology has enabled all national security agencies and military branches to expand their surveillance capabilities. They can closely monitor the activities of American citizens as well as events in other countries. Meanwhile, state and city law enforcement authorities use many of the same tools for localized surveillance. So do private investigators—and, to a lesser but growing extent, private citizens. Here are some examples of organizations, most of them governmental, that use electronic surveillance.

America's Secret Sentry

The agency ultimately charged with protecting America's information secrets is the National Security Agency (NSA). Historian Matthew M. Aid has referred to it as America's "secret sentry." He chronicles its origins and the nature of its work during and since the Cold War in his book *The Secret Sentry: The Untold History of the National Security Agency.*

The glass façade of NSA headquarters in Fort Meade, Maryland, falsely suggests a theme of transparency.

By most accounts, the National Security Agency is one of the most tightly secretive government agencies in the world, if not the most secretive. Insiders and journalists joke that NSA stands for "No Such Agency." Many Americans are unaware of its very existence. In a 2014 *Saturday Evening Post* article about the NSA's history, Michael X. Heiligenstein explains, "As you might expect from an intelligence organization, the National Security Agency has always done its best to avoid unwanted scrutiny from the American public."

Heiligenstein points out that "it isn't really news that the NSA has been spying on people here in our own country. As a matter of fact, that's precisely their job, and has been since President Harry Truman ordered the NSA into existence in 1952."

While the NSA did not become an official government agency until 1952, its origins can be traced to thirty-five years earlier. During World I (1914–1918), the US government created the Cipher Bureau of Military Intelligence to intercept and decipher messages to and from Germany and its allies. After the war, the bureau continued to operate. It monitored telephone and telegraph messages that were exchanged among governmental and other parties in various countries. President Herbert Hoover closed the bureau in 1929, having decided that such surveillance was unnecessary in peacetime.

By then, however, a related project was in the works. The US Army was setting up the Signal Intelligence Service (SIS). The discovery and deciphering of enemy messages and codes by SIS officers proved vital in World War II, especially in the Pacific theater of operations against Japan. The service also employed Native Americans, most famously the Navajos in the Pacific, to transmit messages in their languages that foreign agents could not understand. In 1952, President Truman combined US military signals intelligence efforts into one entity, the National Security Agency.

The National Security Agency shares information with security agencies in other countries. The exact nature and extent of its collaborations are confidential. One known alliance has existed among the NSA and intelligence organizations in the United Kingdom, Canada, Australia, and New Zealand since the early years of the Cold War. They are known collectively as the Five Eyes. Originally, their aim was to monitor communications exchanged by the Soviet Union and its satellite communist regimes in Eastern Europe. In time, their surveillance system reportedly began to be used for spying on other countries, organizations, and individuals.

In the early years, the NSA and its predecessors were limited to surveilling letters, phone calls, telegrams, and personal meetings between suspected enemy agents. The telephone, the telegraph machine, and the wireless telegraph

President Harry Truman (*fourth from right*), pictured here with his cabinet, authorized the creation of the National Security Agency in 1952.

(radio) were the only technologies in place, and these were easily monitored. In the twenty-first century, surveillance technology extends to extremes never imagined during World War I. The NSA and other government entities can eavesdrop on phone conversations, radio broadcasts, and transmissions between terrorist operatives at home and abroad.

Today, much of the NSA's surveillance technology is digital. The agency monitors global information using what have been dubbed **supercomputers**. Its data-gathering systems span the world via the internet and reach beyond Earth's atmosphere to satellites in orbit.

Central Intelligence Agency

The Central Intelligence Agency (CIA) was born when President Franklin D. Roosevelt created an Office of Strategic Services (OSS) after the US entered World War II. The OSS was tasked with collecting and analyzing information that might be important to the war effort.

Although the OSS and similar organizations were disbanded after the war, President Harry S. Truman recognized a need for a centralized intelligence agency even in peaceful times. The modern-day CIA was established by the National Security Act passed in 1947. The Central Intelligence Agency was assigned to coordinate all national intelligence and security activities.

In the current century, cutting-edge technology naturally is vital to the agency's effectiveness. It is used for surveillance as well as communications.

Federal Bureau of Investigation

The FBI was organized unofficially in 1908 by Charles Bonaparte, the US attorney general. Bonaparte brought together a team of thirty-four special agents to work specifically for the Department of Justice; until then, the department had been forced to rely on help by investigative officers from other government departments. In its first decades, the growing agency was noted for probing the activities of crime syndicates, corrupt politicians, and **anarchists**. In time, it became the primary force investigating multiple categories of federal crimes. Its mission is "to protect the American people and uphold the Constitution of the United States."

Since the beginning of the twenty-first century, the bureau has been increasingly active in combatting terrorism and cybercrime. Advanced technologies, including those used for surveillance, are essential in its efforts.

ATF

The federal Bureau of Alcohol, Tobacco, Firearms and Explosives (ATF) is involved in some of the same investigations as the FBI. As its name implies, though, the bureau's focus is on crimes related to those four areas.

Among ATF personnel are intelligence research specialists. Their job description defines them as professionals who are trained to "collect, evaluate, analyze and extract information from various sources for national and international investigations involving terrorist activities, arson rings, and traditional and non-traditional organized crime groups, and compile it into analytical reports and graphs." Among other tasks, they collect and analyze phone records and digital data of suspicious organizations.

Border Patrol

The Border Patrol is now part of US Customs and Border Protection, a branch of the Department of Homeland Security. Established in 1924, it originally was staffed by only 450 officers. They were tasked with preventing illegal immigration and smuggling. That is still the overall objective, but since the terror attacks of September 11, 2001, the agency has shifted its focus to the "detection, apprehension and/or deterrence of terrorists and terrorist weapons," according to its mission statement.

"Line watch" is a critical function. Border Patrol officers from covert positions maintain round-the-clock surveillance of land borders. They look for "terrorists, undocumented aliens, and smugglers of aliens." Much of their surveillance is conducted from the air, using planes, helicopters, and drones. On the ground, they perform traffic checks and observation. Among their technology tools are television systems triggered by electronic sensors.

State and Local Government Surveillance

At the local and state levels, surveillance technologies have been used for the better part of a century by police and

Highway patrol agencies began using speed-detection technology regularly in the 1940s.

highway patrol officers. They also are used by investigative divisions and by special units such as wildlife officers.

The most common objective of surveillance technology at the local level is traffic law enforcement. Electronic traffic monitoring devices are used in cities around the globe. In some countries, speed control cameras are artistically camouflaged.

To maintain safety on streets and highways, speed control is essential. Statistics are compelling. The National Highway Traffic Safety Administration reported that 35,092 Americans died in traffic accidents in 2015. According to the Insurance Institute for Highway Safety, speed has been a factor in about 30 percent of highway fatalities each year since 2005.

Police and highway patrol officers initially based speeding arrests on visual observations and reckoning. **Radar** and cameras were tools that enabled them to apprehend violators and prove their guilt. As early as 1905, a patent was obtained for a camera that could calculate the speed of a passing vehicle. It took time-stamped images at the start and end points of a measured section of road. Decades went by, however, before effective traffic cameras were put into service by police departments.

In the late 1940s, early radar guns began to enable police to measure the speed of a passing vehicle accurately. Later, state transportation agencies were equipped with more sophisticated movement sensor devices and speed-monitoring cameras. Patrol cars equipped with speed detection technology now can determine the speed of a vehicle traveling in either direction. Sensors in modern traffic monitoring devices can determine additional factors such as vehicle occupancy and emission information.

Besides traffic monitoring and enforcement, state and local police use surveillance technology for purposes similar to those of federal agencies. These include electronic monitoring of public properties and areas with high crime rates. Detectives on **stakeouts** use various devices to monitor and document the movements of criminal suspects and persons of interest.

Surveillance by Private Investigators

Private investigators (PIs, or "private eyes") are detectives who generally work on cases that are outside the responsibility of government police agencies. They use some of the same surveillance technology as regular police. Parties in divorce proceedings may hire PIs to find and document evidence of the spouse's infidelity, abuse, false claims, or commandeering of joint property. Private investigators contribute evidence in child custody battles. Parents and families hire independent agents to find missing children. Family members often enlist investigators if they suspect child or elder abuse by relatives or caregivers, or theft by maintenance or housekeeping personnel.

Some PIs specialize in insurance fraud. Insurance companies and employers hire them to obtain evidence that a client or worker's illness or injury claims are exaggerated if not altogether false.

Sometimes crime victims or their families hire private detectives to investigate more thoroughly if they feel frustrated by the lack of progress by police investigators. They may engage a PI to continue probing when police cease active investigation on a mystery that remains unsolved after many years.

Weather satellites keep an eye on Earth and send back a lot of valuable information.

CHAPTER 2

Benefits of Government and Civilian Surveillance

For thousands of years, criminals have committed and gotten away with every sort of malicious act for the simple reason that their crimes were not witnessed and could never be proved. Savage murders, major and minor thefts, vengeful or wanton destruction of property, swindling, **sedition** and **espionage**, cruel mistreatment of others—basically, every category of crime committed today has been committed throughout history.

But today, the likelihood of a crime going unpunished is dwindling. The reason is the great advance of surveillance technology and methods. Twenty-first-century technology equips government agencies, small and large businesses, and private citizens with the ability to detect criminal activity and protect assets. Surveillance devices range from motion sensors to spy cameras to computers. They function from distances of only a few feet or thousands of miles.

Surveillance Technology in Sky and Space

Long-range surveillance was the ultimate incentive for putting the first satellites into orbit in the 1950s. The world superpowers and smaller governments alike considered it vital for defense to constantly monitor the maneuvers of armies and navies of different nations. People never have been the only subject of sky and space surveillance, however. Satellite sensors also can provide scientific details about the composition and quality of Earth's land and water areas as well as its atmosphere. Meteorologists, geologists, environmentalists, and ecologists increasingly have relied on satellite surveillance data in their research.

Most of the pro/con debate over the deployment of satellites and manned spacecraft for observation purposes revolves around spy technology. However, some of the beneficial surveillance and monitoring that's executed from outer space has nothing to do with global politics or military maneuvering. One important user of cutting-edge surveillance technology is the National Oceanic and Atmospheric Administration (NOAA).

NOAA weather satellites are part of the administration's network of air, ground, and sea stations and antennas. As NOAA describes at its website, "Our satellites are part of

Fast Fact

Scientists in the mid-1940s began developing the concept of gathering weather and climate information from space. Early vehicles launched in 1959 were too flawed to obtain significant data. The first operational weather satellite, *TIROS-1*, was sent aloft on April 1, 1960.

a worldwide constellation that supports forecasting around the globe." Weather satellites are crucial for providing up-to-the-minute forecasts and other information about active and developing storm systems. The weather administration has been gleaning data from satellites for more than half a century.

Ground stations and antennas in widespread locations provide constant control of the satellites. They ensure that the craft precisely maintain their assigned orbits. Meanwhile, they receive, process, and distribute a steady flow of information about active and developing storm systems and environmental activities and trends. This information is vital to weather forecasters, emergency response agencies, and climate scientists.

NOAA's modern satellites are extremely sensitive. The administration has developed different types of satellites for difference surveillance and monitoring purposes. The sophistication of NOAA's spacecraft exemplifies the advances of twenty-first-century satellite surveillance technology.

In charge of scheduling and data management is NOAA's Office of Satellite and Product Operations (OSPO). The office monitors two types of satellites. From the ground, a geostationary operational environmental satellite (GOES) seems motionless, always in the same position. That's because the satellite orbits in the same direction in which Earth rotates, at the same relative rate. Geostationary satellites travel above the equator at an altitude of about 22,300 miles (35,800 kilometers). An advantage of this class of satellite is that tracking antennas on the ground can be faced permanently toward the satellite's same aerial position rather than rotating. Geostationary satellites use light sensors to detect even the slightest changes in ocean temperatures and currents.

Another category of weather satellite is the polar operational environmental satellite (POES). This type of craft makes approximately fourteen **polar** orbits of Earth each day at a height of about 520 miles (837 kilometers). Because Earth is rotating, a POES can survey a different part of the planet in each orbit. NOAA keeps one POES in the sky constantly. The information it gleans is supplemented by data obtained by a similar satellite operated by the European Organisation for the Exploitation of Meteorological Satellites. These satellites measure details about clouds, precipitation, humidity, ocean surface temperatures, volcanic activity, forest fires, vegetation, and other environmental elements. Information transmitted from them can be used in search and rescue operations.

Weather satellites are important instruments for accurately analyzing the effects of climate change. They have shown that worldwide sea levels on average have been rising by 0.114 inches (2.9 millimeters, or about the thickness of three pennies) annually in recent years. In 2014, the average sea level measurement was 2.63 inches (67 mm) higher than the average in 1993. Scientists consider rising sea levels, which are caused by melting polar ice, to be one of the most dramatic results of global warming.

Military, Police, and Commercial Sky Surveillance

Reconnaissance satellites and high-flying airplanes operated by military and government intelligence entities can render images of subjects far below them in astounding detail, day and night. Penetrating clouds, they can watch the movements of individuals, see inside certain buildings, and even identify chemical substances.

Besides satellites, military branches and security agencies make regular use of airplanes, helicopters, and drones for surveillance—as do scientific agencies and institutions. An example from the early years of the War on Terror illustrates the extraordinary power of this type of technology. A special forces drone flying above the desert in Yemen launched a missile to destroy an SUV on a dusty road below. Inside the car were six al-Qaeda terrorist suspects, including a leader considered one of the most dangerous men in the region. The missile launch was activated from a US military base in Virginia.

The mission demonstrated a coordination of multiple surveillance technologies at work. Army intelligence officers had been able to hack the prime suspect's mobile phone. Without his knowledge, they remotely turned on the phone while he motored along the desert road. The phone signal provided the missile-armed drone with the precise tracking information needed to carry out the launch.

Police agencies frequently blend technologies when investigating and locating fugitives. On a far less dramatic level, so do business enterprises, for the benefit of consumers. For example, when you search the internet with your mobile phone for the location of a small business address, you likely immediately will be shown written instructions for how to get there from your location, a photo of the building, the phone number, hours of operation, name of the owner, and more.

Putting Drones to Good Use

Proponents of drone technology cite numerous ways unpiloted aerial vehicles (UAVs) are benefiting society apart from police and military surveillance missions. Public service agencies have used them in search operations and even in relief and rescue efforts, dropping in medicine, food, and water to victims injured or stranded in isolated places. Conservation scientists use unpiloted craft to monitor the status of imperiled wildlife species. Large farming operations are using drones to check the health of their crops; they can identify portions of a broad field that require more water or fertilizer. Firefighters have flown drones over out-of-control fires to help determine the best strategies and tactics. National Oceanic and Atmospheric Administration weather surveillance planes sometimes operate in conjunction with low-flying UAVs equipped with atmospheric sensors.

Many of the aerial scenes we see in films and television commercials were taken by drone cameras. This is much more cost-efficient for the production company than engaging a helicopter or airplane. Drones are used to inspect buildings and heavy equipment from heights and angles that would be very dangerous for a human to access. Claims adjusters for insurance companies in many cases are able to estimate damages and calculate repair or replacement costs without visiting the scene, using only images and video footage captured by drones.

Other drone uses are in developmental stages. Amazon is experimenting with using UAVs to deliver parcels to online shoppers. If the system proves effective, a small box or package could be delivered to certain purchasers' addresses not overnight but in a matter of hours. Walmart likewise is investigating the potential for deliveries by UAVs. (It may be noteworthy that 70 percent of Americans live within 5 miles (8 km) of a Walmart, according to retail research.) Domino's and other restaurant chains have tested the delivery of take-out orders via drone.

Meanwhile, internet companies such as Google and Facebook are contemplating the use of high-altitude drones to provide broadband access to people in remote regions who presently have no service. This technology, like some of the other projects in development, may be years in arriving.

Already, UAVs—even those flown by children and adult hobbyists—have astonishing sophistication and powers. Many of the controllers, even for inexpensive models, have first-person-viewing (FPV) screens. From a distance, perhaps out of sight of the aircraft, the pilot sees on the display panel what the drone video camera is seeing. Some drones are so small that, flying at heights of only a few yards, they are difficult to see from the ground. Even units that small and inconspicuous may be controlled with FPV capability.

Not all drones are aircraft. Police and military special units on the ground direct wheel-borne drones to investigate buildings considered too dangerous for human forces to enter. Naval units use underwater drone craft for surveillance and investigations as well as to clear mines, carry out combat strikes, and transport supplies. These craft include remotely operated vehicles (ROVs), which are tethered to the command craft, and unmanned undersea vehicles (UUVs), which are untethered.

Apart from military purposes, UUVs have been used to locate wreckage of planes that crash at sea. Remote environmental monitoring units (REMUS drones) dive deep to perform oceanographic and meteorological surveillance.

Surveillance on the Ground

As technological surveillance progressed in the second half of the twentieth century, only a small fraction of Americans ever were subjected to police or government phone taps. Their first encounters with surveillance tech involved traffic violations. From then until now, drivers have chafed when caught by speed monitoring technology.

In the controversy over highway speeding surveillance, authorities have a strong rationale for using it. The stated purpose of speed detection equipment is to slow traffic to a safer pace. Typically, traffic officers allow drivers to exceed the limit to a certain degree—mainly because there are far more speeders than officers can apprehend. They focus on stopping the most egregious violators, for example:

- Those driving 10 to 20 miles per hour (16 to 32 kmh) faster than the posted limit.

- Those driving fast in school and hospital crossing and entrance/exit zones.

- Those driving fast through residential neighborhoods.

- Those driving fast on dangerous curves and hills.

Their argument is undeniable: excessive speed kills. State highway departments use accident statistics to determine where to focus surveillance technology for speed control.

Today, traffic surveillance devices not only can determine a vehicle's speed; they can record video of the vehicle and in many instances zoom close enough to identify the license tag. The speeder, reckless driver, or hit-and-run culprit might exit the scene at liberty, only to be greeted at the home door shortly after by officers with an arrest **warrant**, or to receive notification of a fine in the mail.

Airport and Industrial Screening

People entering the boarding areas of airports must pass through security checkpoints. Several forms of surveillance technology are used. US Transportation and Security Administration officers use walk-through metal detectors and imaging devices to detect weapons, explosives, or prohibited electronics hidden in clothing. Individuals unable to pass through imaging monitors because of medical reasons undergo pat-down screening.

Baggage passes through separate screening. Officers can see the contents inside bags, looking out for potentially dangerous items or ordinary devices in which dangerous small components might be concealed.

Airport security was intensified when criminals in the 1960s and 1970s skyjacked numerous jetliners and smaller planes for different purposes: extortion, militant operations, flight from justice, etc. Most people agree the need for sophisticated airport surveillance is real, especially in the aftermath of the September 2001 terrorist hijackings of commercial flights that culminated in the slaughter of thousands of Americans and foreigners. Citizens are willing to tolerate longer boarding delays.

Similar screening technology is used by Amazon and other online order fulfillment companies. When employees exit the merchandise storage area on break or at the conclusion of a shift, they must pass through gates fitted with electronic sensors much like those used at airports. The objective is to catch employees who may try to leave the building with stolen electronics and other small goods concealed in their clothing.

A typical incident at a southeastern distribution center illustrates how this works. Loss-prevention agents monitoring different areas of the building via overhead video cameras noticed a picker—an employee roving the aisles gathering products for order processing—acting suspiciously. Studying his movements, they saw him appear to slip small items behind his belt band.

At the next shift break, the loss prevention chief and security supervisor watched quietly as employees exited through the screening gates. Predictably, the suspect set off an electronic gate alarm as he passed. He routinely stepped aside to allow an inspector to pass a hand wand over his body. The electronic wand detected metal at his midsection. The man casually drew a few coins from a pocket, pretending he had forgotten to remove them before passing through the gate.

In previous thefts (video reviews showed evidence he had been stealing for weeks), screening officers had assumed pocket change, keys, or a fingernail file were the reason why he triggered the metal detectors, and they had dismissed him. This time, the supervisors escorted him to a private office. A more thorough wanding detected small, expensive computer gaming articles concealed in his underwear.

Business and Municipal Camera Installations

Businesses and municipalities cite numerous benefits of constant surveillance. The obvious one is to record criminal activities. Surveillance videos have provided crucial leads for police in identifying and apprehending suspects. They record strong evidence for criminal trials.

Video footage also can help protect a business against a fabricated lawsuit. Slip-and-fall injury scams have been perpetrated for generations. Now, with obscure cameras recording every minute of activity at an alleged accident scene, con artists are encountering a formidable obstacle. By the same token, recorded video can help legitimate accident victims prove their claims to dubious insurance appraisers. It is difficult for an accident policy insurer to deny a claim if the cause of a serious injury is captured on a video camera.

The knowledge that a site may be under electronic surveillance is itself a deterrent to criminals and false claim plotters. Bank staff are trained to surrender the money a robber demands without resistance. They know that in most robberies today, police can identify and quickly arrest the bandit, thanks to surveillance technology.

Retail businesses of all sizes, from convenience stores to supermarkets and large department stores, use surveillance cameras to thwart shoplifters. At larger stores, in-house security staff maintain live surveillance of shoplifters, particularly scrutinizing aisles where items of prime interest to shoplifters are displayed. In some situations, shoplifters are detected and apprehended immediately. If they escape with stolen goods, video evidence can be useful for identifying them later and proving their actions.

Employee fraud reportedly accounts for billions of dollars annually in losses to corporations. Stealing from the company is not the only form of misdeed. Lazy and manipulative employees may never steal physical valuables from their employers, but they steal time. In numerous studies, thousands of workers have acknowledged they spend considerable time at work (several hours a day, in many cases) on office computers playing games, surfing the internet, chatting online, and shopping. Some use their employers' computers to establish, expand, and promote their own side businesses—and get paid for the time they spend doing that.

Surveillance videos can expose such behavior and help demonstrate reasonable grounds for firing. Increasingly, large-scale employers and even small businesses are requiring workers to sign policies acknowledging that their workplace activities are subject to monitoring.

Police Use of Technology

A 911 call in Fresno, California, in January 2016 sent police rushing to the scene of a scary encounter in which a man with a gun was loudly threatening his ex-girlfriend. From a neighbor, the emergency call operator got the attacker's name. Entering the name into a software system called Beware while officers were en route, authorities were able to instantly search arrest records, property information, social media posts, and the deep web to determine the assailant's potential threat score. Finding that he was linked to gangs and had been convicted on a firearm charge, they deemed it prudent to dispatch a police negotiator to the site.

This incident illustrates the sophistication law enforcement departments have acquired through technology. Rapid database searches—in that case, scanning literally billions of data bytes—combined with an elaborate arsenal of other tech tools are extremely useful to modern police. Besides helping protect citizens and officers, database surveillance helps police prevent crimes, locate and arrest criminal suspects, identify terrorists, and gather evidence in criminal cases.

A police helicopter provides an investigation team details not evident to officers on the ground.

Law enforcement officials consider surveillance technology essential if their agencies are to serve citizens effectively. In large cities, operators receive more than one thousand 911 calls every day. Typically, dozens of gangs are at large. Serious crimes ranging from shootings and robberies to domestic assaults occur constantly. Surveillance devices enable police to document crimes, identify the people involved, and track fleeing suspects. Technology has also allowed each patrol car to be a Wi-Fi hotspot so officers can connect all devices to the internet. Adaptive mobile computing helps consolidate all the devices an officer may use into a single device that can be carried anywhere.

Police technology and techniques have changed dramatically during the past fifty years. In the twenty-first century, it has become a popular academic concentration for students pursuing a secondary degree. Police tech is now a science. Local, state, federal, and international law enforcement agencies share technologies and personnel. Every day, videos, intercepted voice and digital communications, and other data collected by authorities in one country are made available to their counterparts abroad in the common interest of justice, security, and safety. The types and sophistication of police surveillance technology vary among countries as a result of economic, cultural, political, geographical, and population differences. Nonetheless, most nations' law enforcement agencies are able to share findings with foreign police.

Surveillance tools allow police to monitor the movements of groups that assemble in public. Gatherings include peaceful events such as holiday parades, nonviolent protests, and memorial observances. Surveillance helps ensure that the proceedings remain safe and orderly. Meanwhile, surveillance enables authorities to keep an eye on potentially unlawful activities such as the movements of known gangs and the actions of belligerent rioters.

Uniformed and plain-clothes officers have used short-wave radio communications for almost a century to report on activities they observe while on patrol or in investigations. Since the 1980s, they have used cell phones and **pagers**. More recently, they've relied on smartphones and tablet computers for the same kinds of communication—with far greater technical capabilities.

Audio surveillance tools became commonplace in the early 1900s. Police have installed phone taps and have wired indoor and outdoor locations with hidden microphones. They also have wired undercover agents with voice monitors and recorders to capture conversations between the agents and underworld contacts. More recently, they have used video

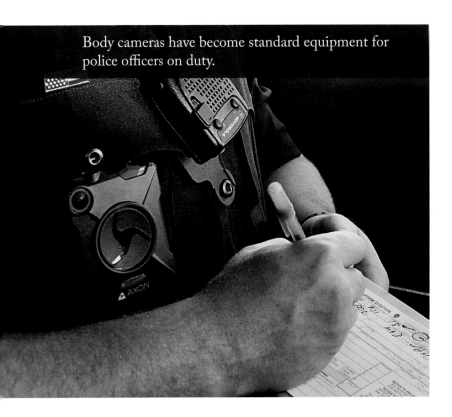

Body cameras have become standard equipment for police officers on duty.

cameras for similar purposes. Powerful wireless recorders today may be so tiny that they can be installed anywhere, even inside handheld devices. They are practically impossible to see unless a professional technician knows just what to look for.

Binoculars, telescopes, and cameras and video cameras fitted with telephoto lenses are standard equipment in most sizable police departments in the United States. Certain police units and military forces are equipped with night-vision goggles and binoculars. With closed-circuit television cameras (CCTVs), officers in remote control centers can peer through windows and even under doors of buildings suspected to be occupied by dangerous individuals. They can see what's inside even if a room is in total darkness. Police are also wearing a heads-up display, a transparent display screen that allows them to view information without looking away from what they are watching. Officers can request information verbally and then see the search results on their display screens. These devices can contain face-recognition technology, one reason regulators are concerned about sales to civilians not involved in law enforcement.

Across some large cities, hundreds of obscure police cameras are installed. Hundreds more are worn by officers on patrol. Monitor operators at headquarters can zoom in on suspicious activity at any of the locations. In addition, they may have access to security cameras at schools and other public facilities, as well as at private businesses.

Police also use cyber technology for a variety of surveillance purposes. With computer trawling systems, for example, police can scan social media posts for evidence and clues suggesting potential criminal activity. Social media posts that originated in a concentrated area can help police predict the location of criminal networks and of illegal activity, and they can send officers to a region to prevent the activity.

Private Eye Technology

"The private investigator is in the business of gathering and selling information." So writes Sheila L. Stephens, a private investigator and former special agent for the US Bureau of Alcohol, Tobacco, Firearms and Explosives, in *The Everything Private Investigation Book*. "In order to do this, she relies on specific tools that are designed to uncover particular evidence."

Most private investigators are former police detectives. They have years of experience, they thoroughly understand the laws, and they are well familiar with much of the same equipment issued to police officers.

Smartphones and other wireless mobile computer devices are essential components of a private investigator's surveillance tool kit. They use high-end cameras and video cameras with zoom lenses and night-vision capability. The microphones they employ to record conversations are supersensitive.

Private investigators sometimes wear concealed audio and video (AV) recording devices such as tiny **camcorders**

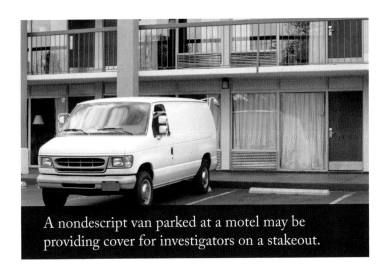

A nondescript van parked at a motel may be providing cover for investigators on a stakeout.

mounted in the barrels of writing pens or attached inconspicuously to belts or lapels. Modern-day concealable AV instruments are extremely powerful. They can render high-resolution photographs and videos and clearly record conversations taking place several yards from the investigator's position. Recordings automatically are date/time-stamped, which is critical if they are to be entered as evidence in court.

While private investigators use surveillance equipment similar to that of police, they use it for different purposes. As their job description suggests, PIs are hired by private individuals and businesses, including many insurance companies. Their assignments are to conduct investigations which, while they may involve civil and even criminal wrongdoings, typically are left alone by police agencies, which have broader responsibilities.

An example is medical fraud. People are entitled to compensation if an injury they sustain on the job or in an accident causes them to lose the ability to work or impairs their mobility and quality of life. Too often, victims pretend to have disabilities that don't exist or exaggerate injuries in order to receive more money. For some, a minor accident becomes a lifelong gold mine if the claimant can convince doctors and, in turn, insurers that the condition is far more serious than it is. Essentially, healthy fraudsters receive salary compensation for many years without having to return to work.

Professional criminals carry out personal injury scams. For example, a personal injury ring may cleverly orchestrate an "accident." One or more of its members pretends to be seriously hurt. An innocent party is sued for injuries. The same gang may be back at work in a different state within days, staging a similar con.

In the end, the targeted individuals or insurance companies must pay damages. Often, judgment is rendered after a trial in which someone conspiring with the ring gives false testimony against the scam victim.

Insurance companies that pay injury benefit claims naturally want assurance that the victim is truly incapacitated or traumatized. So do scammed individuals who may find themselves personally liable for paying out of pocket. Only rarely do police investigate; if they do, it usually is when they learn that a "victim" has a criminal record for such offenses. If wronged parties hope to win justice, they must turn to private investigators to try to obtain proof of fraud.

Gathering the legally necessary proof may take weeks, months, or years. Private detectives employ a number of surveillance devices and tactics. Video cameras, voice recorders, and drones commonly are used by PIs, as are telephoto and night-vision equipment. In recent years, detectives commonly have used hidden body cameras for close-up surveillance. A pen camera, for instance, looks (and usually functions) like a writing pen, but a small video camera

A spy pen, with its camera just above the clip, can record images and conversations several yards away.

Depending on Data

One key to success in police surveillance efforts in the twenty-first century is the availability to all agencies of a comprehensive, reliable central database of information. An important related factor is cooperation among law enforcement entities at different levels and in different locales.

The National Crime Information Center (NCIC) detailed a recent case in which an agent with the US Forest Service requested help from the center. The agent, stationed in the Midwest, was involved in a drug trafficking investigation. What was needed was a search of purged NCIC data possibly linked to the case. Searches turned up a connection between certain persons and vehicles. "This connection assisted in locating and identifying suspects associated with the case, and was invaluable in following the suspects' activities in relation to moving people, money, and products," the NCIC reported.

At the time that police announced details of the investigation, twenty individuals had been convicted of charges concerned with the case. The search results also led officers to identify additional suspects and discover further details about the trafficking ring. Agents confiscated an estimated $1 million worth of property, some of it stolen, as well as vehicles, firearms, drugs, and cash.

Since its creation in 1967 as a function of the Federal Bureau of Investigation, the NCIC has seen its stores of computer data mushroom. This has enabled it to expand its focus areas. In recent years, it has added the Violent Person File. The information it contains alerts police if an individual at an active response scene has been hostile to law enforcement personnel in the past.

Another new data category is the NICS Denied Transaction File. The NICS is the FBI's National Instant Criminal Background Check System. The file contains records of people who have been denied the purchase of a handgun after failing a background check.

is fitted inside the barrel, with a tiny lens and microphone mounted outside, above the clip. Pen cameras render high-resolution color videos and clearly record conversations taking place a considerable distance away.

Like police, private detectives rely heavily on computer research. They search online for addresses, phone numbers, and other essential details. They also look into social media for profiles and posts that give clues about the interests, friends, favorite hangouts, etc., of persons of interest.

Private investigators employ these surveillance methods to gather evidence in other types of cases. A common assignment for a PI is to observe and document the activities and whereabouts of someone suspected of marital infidelity. Is the suspect often seen making a rendezvous at a romantic café with someone who is not the spouse? Or is the suspect seen frequently entering that person's home or apartment? In order to glean such evidence, a private detective or team may stake out certain locations day after day, night after night, with no result. When suspicious incidents are observed, photos and videos obtained from the stakeout vehicle or secluded ground position document the date and time.

Private detectives also are involved in child custody cases, in which the behavior of one of the custodians comes into question. Parents sometimes engage investigators to check on the activities of problem teens.

Data Gathering

Beginning in the second half of the twentieth century, a new form of surveillance technology was added to visual and audio devices. In the modern era of computers and, in particular, the internet and other connected networks online, the gathering and analysis of personal information allows organizations and companies to track and understand an individual's habits and interests. Data surveillance is done by government agencies, retailers, marketers, and sometimes by friends.

Law enforcement agencies were among the first to recognize the usefulness of information that is exchanged and stored on computers. Federal and state law enforcement agencies as well as county, local, and tribal police departments created and began to build computer databases containing details about US and foreign citizens.

The Federal Bureau of Investigation established the National Crime Information Center in 1967. The government by that point had begun to store immense volumes of information on early **mainframe computers.** The NCIC compiled records from police agencies all over the country, making the information available to all agencies. This was a profound improvement in tracking criminals who had records in multiple jurisdictions and in tracing the interstate transport of stolen goods.

An FBI agent (*left*) and intelligence analyst learn electronic investigation skills.

The first reported "hit" obtained from the new computer system came almost immediately, in May 1967. A New York City police officer, suspicious of a parked car, radioed its license number to headquarters. About a minute later, he was informed the car recently had been stolen in Boston.

Among other records, the database today contains criminal mugshots; fingerprints; the numbers of stolen vehicles, licenses, firearms, and financial securities; a national sex offender registry; and information about missing persons, suspected terrorists, gang members, immigration violators, foreign fugitives, and convicted criminals being supervised on **probation** and **parole**.

System information exchanges occur in a two-way design. The FBI provides a computer server with connections to specified contact points at other federal criminal justice agencies and at agencies in every US state, Puerto Rico, the US Virgin Islands, and Guam, as well as in Canada. Those agencies have smaller database systems of their own. All are linked, providing common access to any connected source files by any agency. Each agency is responsible for altering and eventually removing the records that it enters.

Before computer searching and analysis was available, it was difficult for police in any given locale to recognize relationships between past and current incidents in different states and countries that involved a particular suspect. Such information could be pieced together, but only if an investigator recalled related details. The "memory" of a computer database system, by contrast, is practically encyclopedic.

As technology has improved steadily in recent decades, access to NCIC files has quickened. At a typical traffic stop, the police officer can check the database and learn instantly if the vehicle is stolen or if the driver is a fugitive. (That information alone does not justify an immediate arrest; further inquiries must be made to ensure the NCIC information is current and accurate.) For many file types, the average response time is a fraction of a second.

The quantity of records and the number of information requests at the NCIC is mindboggling. A record was set on July 28, 2016, when 17,492,427 transactions were processed by the NCIC. At its website, the center describes its data pool as "the lifeline of law enforcement—an electronic clearinghouse of crime data that can be tapped into by virtually every criminal justice agency nationwide, 24 hours a day, 365 days a year."

Agencies in other nations and regional **confederacies** also maintain digital databases. Most notable is the International Criminal Police Organization (ICPO, commonly known as Interpol), a network of agencies involving 190 countries. The Schengen Information System (SIS) serves the European Union. The Royal Canadian Mounted Police (RCMP) is the legendary national police force of Canada. The Federal

Security Service of the Russian Federation (FSB) is the successor of the infamous KGB (Committee for State Security) in the former Soviet Union. Australia is represented by the Australian Federal Police (AFP). Such organizations share among themselves information about terrorists and other criminals, stolen goods, and missing persons. Interpol keeps a voluminous collection of fingerprints and DNA profiles, which can be accessed by police agencies worldwide.

Digital information databases are used not just to survey criminal activities but to aid police and other emergency responders in their performance of many different public services. For example, computerized records enable them to quickly identify and notify next of kin of victims involved in serious accidents. Computer data help them pinpoint physical addresses, determine where the nearest response units are positioned, and identify and communicate with property owners in emergencies. They also identify owners of vehicles, boats, guns, and other valuable items, facilitating the return of stolen goods.

Digital files are invaluable for finding missing persons. In recent years, more than six hundred thousand missing persons annually have been entered into the NCIC's Missing Person File, which was created in 1975. Their information is kept on file until the person is found or the local police agency that entered the name cancels the entry. Missing persons include runaways, abductees, people missing in the wake of a mass catastrophe, and people with mental or physical disabilities who are unable to identify themselves or their guardians.

Happily, more than 90 percent of missing persons eventually are found or identified and return to normal life. But as of the end of 2014, the NCIC still had approximately eighty-five thousand active missing person records.

Unobtrusive and hidden camera installations monitor traffic, even capturing license tags and other details.

CHAPTER 3

Objections to Surveillance Technology

I n twenty-first-century America, you might find a bill in your mailbox from the state motor vehicle department if you recently failed to pay when accessing a toll road. Your vehicle image and license number were caught by a surveillance camera. Most honest drivers would admit—begrudgingly, perhaps—that this form of surveillance is legitimate. It's a simple, harmless tool for enforcing a traffic law.

But what if, while traveling the interstate at the speed limit (or only slightly faster), you occasionally accelerate by as much as 10 miles per hour (16 kmh) in order to pass a slow truck on an upgrade or to relieve a traffic backup in your lane? And what if, in that brief moment, on that particular short stretch of highway, you're caught speeding by a traffic surveillance installation?

In that situation, you might begin to question modern surveillance technology and its use. You would have lots of company.

Dodging Speed Traps

Popular opposition to speed traps was one of the earliest complaints about the use of surveillance techniques and technologies by law enforcement agencies. The somber slogan "Speed Kills" spread across the United States as automobiles became the most common mode of transportation and accidents multiplied. Police in the mid-twentieth century began using radar and other technologies to document speeding incidents.

However, many municipal governments and agencies also began leveraging speed control to improve their finances. Municipal leaders in countless small towns realized that speeding fines could provide substantial **revenue** for their modest, strained budgets. Only so much income can be derived from taxing a small population. By catching speeders, governments can add thousands of dollars to their coffers every month.

"Speed traps" became anathema to motorists passing through those towns—and to many town citizens. Thousands of towns, communities, and stretches of highway acquired reputations as radar zones. Word spread far and wide. Travelers learned to avoid those routes. Some citizens feared the damage being done to their towns' images was not worth the steady income from traffic fines. Apparently, however, most town government administrations calculated that income from speeders more than compensated for any loss in local tourism.

Angry motorists reacted with countermeasures. Some installed radar detectors and blocking devices in their cars. Those instruments were banned in some states (and their effectiveness has been questionable). In some instances, vandals went to the extreme of destroying traffic camera installations. Citizens created websites to alert travelers of known hotbeds of traffic surveillance.

That backlash was relatively mild compared to critical causes that have arisen against more sophisticated forms of surveillance technology. Protests target many forms of aerial, ground, and cyber surveillance. Civil libertarians argue, for example, that data-scouring systems such as the Beware program that helps police vet suspects in advance of an arrest may constitute privacy intrusions. They argue that such systems are not subject to public scrutiny and may warrant regulation.

Satellite Issues

An obvious concern with spy satellites is whether they are obtaining images of private individuals or their property. How can citizens be assured how satellite-gathered intelligence is used, or who is using it? It is noteworthy that US government agencies, trusted though they may be, are not the only operators of highly sensitive surveillance satellites.

Privacy is not the only concern of those who challenge the use of satellite technology. A troubling question has been asked almost since the beginning of the satellite era: What happens to craft orbiting Earth when they "die"? Critics worry that the countless satellites launched during the past sixty years pose physical hazards if they malfunction and after they run out of power.

The number of artificial objects in space that no longer are active is unknown, since many of them were launched secretly. As they increase in density, so does the risk of collision either with other spacecraft or with Earth's surface.

Higher-altitude satellites, such as weather satellites circling Earth at altitudes of more than 22,000 miles (35,400 kilometers), typically are thrust even higher, out of

This piece of outer hull of a UK spacecraft was found in Brazil in 2014. Space junk is expected to increase.

ordinary flight paths, after **decommissioning** and are left in orbit as virtual space zombies. The National Oceanic and Atmospheric Administration estimates they may continue to circle Earth silently for hundreds of years. Space agencies can control the demise of many lower-altitude satellites after they are decommissioned. Their orbits gradually are lowered, and as the craft are overtaken by Earth's gravity, the intense heat of reentry effectively disintegrates them. Other vehicles are guided to crash in vast, untraveled ocean regions.

Sometimes, though, artificial space objects crash to Earth unpredictably. In November 2016, a heavy object believed to be part of a Chinese satellite plunged into a jade mining region of Myanmar, shaking nearby buildings. It was approximately 15 feet (4.6 meters) long and cylindrical in shape, about 5 feet (1.5 m) in diameter. The object landed with such force that it bounced 150 feet (46 m) from the initial point of impact.

While no known fatalities have resulted from falling satellite and rocket debris, scientists say satellites and manned spacecraft launched in coming years will be subject to rising probabilities of collisions in space. Already, collisions between satellites and satellite remnants of different nations have occurred. The International Space Station has had to change its orbit path to avoid debris more than a dozen times and actually has been damaged. Even tiny objects can be hazardous because of extreme orbit velocities. A particle of paint once left a chip in a space station window.

Drone Issues

Public outcry against drones flying over residential neighborhoods is hardly surprising. People fear that what they do in private on their own property may be subject to spying by anyone with a drone. Before drones became

Fast Fact

Dr. Hugh Lewis, a UK space scientist, recently told colleagues at the Royal Astronomical Society that space junk poses one of the most serious environmental problems of the twenty-first century. Hundreds of millions of artificial objects, many of them microscopic in size, encircle Earth. The largest deactivated satellite is the size of a double-decker bus.

prevalent, a tall, solid fence or screens generally sufficed to ensure privacy in one's swimming pool or backyard. Not so anymore.

The fundamental problem with drones, privacy advocates point out, is that they can be purchased and flown by practically anyone. For $2,500, $100, or as little as $20, they can be purchased online on the spur of the moment with no questions asked. No flight training is required.

Many (hopefully most) drone pilots, amateurs as well as professionals, have no interest in observing what other people are doing. They simply enjoy developing skills flying a remote-controlled aircraft over different types of terrain, sometimes in challenging weather conditions. Others, though, cannot resist the temptation of social snooping—even if it was not their motive for buying the drone. Who's attending that lively dock party across the lake? What are they drinking? What are they wearing?

In bygone days, meddlers checked up on neighbors by casually strolling past homes, peering into backyards, perhaps ringing the doorbell on some pretext to learn who might be visiting. The only "surveillance" tools they had to assist them were binoculars for zooming in and telephones for sharing gossip. Today, the drone provides inquisitive people with powerful technology for prying.

Such behavior is not illegal, unless some of the gossip is malicious slander. Snooping always has been a part of social behavior that most people find tolerable and even amusing. In the internet age, the situation has changed. Cyberbullies use social media to assault the character of individuals. They leverage information they've discovered and compromising photographs and videos they've obtained to blackmail victims.

From time to time, leery citizens have taken it upon themselves to deal with suspicious drones. Drones have been shot from the skies, resulting in legal action. Solidification of uniform laws governing the adversarial rights of drone owners and antagonists in specific incidents is in the early stage. Unique cause-and-result scenarios continue to emerge.

Public opinion is divided on whether citizens should be entitled to react aggressively to drones, even when the craft hover disturbingly low above someone's property. Privacy proponents believe such drone piloting is intolerable. Although the pilot may claim, for example, to be taking aerial photographs for a real estate firm, no one except the pilot knows what individuals, objects, and activities come into view. No law or regulation can force the drone pilot to disclose or destroy potentially sensitive photos and videos.

Drone pilots counter that accidental surveillance by drones is no different from unintentional aerial viewing by pilots and passengers in piloted aircraft. There can be little doubt that recreational airplane pilots and commercial aerial photographers observe activities from the heights that are not meant for the public eye. The same is true of news, traffic, police, and military helicopter and plane crews. Countless scenes are witnessed inadvertently, activities that are not at all illegal but definitely are intended to be private.

Critics also cite safety issues in the use of drones by citizens who include child pilots with little or questionable parental guidance. For whatever purpose they're used, drones have been known to cause accidents. Drone crashes by experienced pilots are frequent; in the hands of learners, crashes are inestimable. Out-of-control UAVs have damaged property and injured people on the ground. A worst-case scenario, so far unreported, would be an accidental collision between a drone and a low-flying airplane, such as a plane taking off or landing at a small airport. The drones could be sucked into the engines of low-flying jet aircraft, causing them to crash. For that reason, government regulations stipulate a certain distance from airport runways as no-fly zones for drone operators. Amateurs used drones to take photos of wildfires raging in California in 2015, grounding helicopters that were being used to drop water on the flames. There were six cases in California in 2016 in which amateur drones grounded aircraft fighting fires, with the California Department of Forestry and Fire Protection making its first arrest of a drone operator in July 2016.

Skeptics also are wary, for safety reasons, of the testing of drones for non-surveillance purposes such as package and food deliveries. The UAVs primarily would operate over densely populated areas, using low-altitude airspace occupied by traffic and medical helicopters. In major metro areas, already crowded skies would become much more crowded, especially during peak delivery times.

Some safety advocates, as well as civil libertarians, would like to see closer regulation of drone usage. As with all technology fads and movements, consumers buy and embrace the products long before legislators and government regulators have time to debate the issues, formulate usage policies, and pass laws. Lawyers and legislators currently are focusing on the legal ramifications when drones are involved in incidents that could result in civil litigation. Regulators deal with matters of air safety.

Currently, the Federal Aviation Administration requires recreational drone owners to register any unmanned aircraft system (UAS) that weighs more than 0.55 pounds

(0.25 kilograms). Online registration costs five dollars and is valid for three years. Commercial drone pilots must submit more formal paperwork.

Federal aviation regulations stipulate that "no person may operate an aircraft in a careless or reckless manner so as to endanger the life or property of another." Many states have likewise passed laws relating to drones, with new legislation under debate. California, for example, bans photographing a citizen from on or above the person's private property without permission. Wisconsin has made it a crime to fit a weapon onto a nonmilitary drone.

Critics believe current laws do not go far enough. But regardless of how stringent the laws and regulations are made, enforcement will be an obvious problem. Who is to prevent drone operators from doing as they please, especially if the craft is hovering at an undetectable distance from a target site? One state outlaws the use of drones for photographing nude or partially nude individuals; it seems, though, that discovering such an infraction and proving the identity of the malefactor is up to citizens.

Ground Surveillance Issues

Stealthy ground surveillance, like drone surveillance, has raised privacy concerns. Potential scenarios that raise cries of foul are endless. Suppose, for example, you meet an acquaintance in a department store and enter into what turns out to be an extended conversation. The topics are irrelevant; you could be discussing schoolteachers, mutual friends, music, politics, the weather, or perhaps musings along romantic lines.

A short distance away on the same aisle, a young man seems enthralled reading the packaging notes of a popular

This three-dimensional scanner can see through clothes to detect concealed weapons.

product. You assume he's out of hearing. Possibly, though, he is wearing a small, camouflaged bodycam. Regardless of whether the person is a licensed store detective or a mischievous gadget freak, you probably would be uncomfortable if you knew your conversation was being recorded. You certainly would be furious if craftily tampered segments of it were posted on social media and went viral.

Such forms of secretive ground surveillance are one realm of concern. Another is the use of visible surveillance installations, notably electronic screening stations.

While most passengers are willing to undergo electronic screening at airports, some critics say the effectiveness of such screening does not justify the delays, inconvenience, and privacy intrusions. The American Civil Liberties Union at its website posts that the Transportation Security Agency's stationing of security officers to screen passengers for suspicious actions "is based on junk science and is a waste of money." In response to complaints about airport screening technology, the Transportation Safety Administration assures that it does not use X-ray technology (a potential hazard for individuals with certain medical conditions) and that it employs strict privacy standards.

Similar criticism is levied against security stations in major retail shipping facilities. Employees pass through screening whenever they leave the work floor to go home or go on breaks. At certain seasons and times of day, hundreds of employees must walk through screening gates in the space of a few minutes. When one or more of them sets off the electronic alarm—typically for accidentally having pocket change or some other metallic object on their person—they are directed to secondary screening to be bodily wanded. This causes further slowdowns. Employees complain that screening is invasive and costs them much of the time they have available for breaks.

Virtual Surveillance Issues

Most Americans are at least somewhat worried about stolen identity and the loss of privacy in the age of the internet.

Millions have been victimized through compromised personal information and stolen credit card and bank account numbers. Some have lost thousands of dollars. In many instances, it takes years for them to get their credit repaired and their lives back to normal.

What places them at risk is the collection of personal information—particularly financial information—by businesses that keep records on customer purchases, hospitals and doctors' offices that maintain records on patients, and even government agencies that collect and store records of various types. Such databases have proved to be vulnerable to hacking. The advent of social media, where individuals freely share details about themselves, has presented a broad channel for ID thieves.

Besides financial damage, reputational damage is spreading. False negative reports circulated on the internet about individuals and organizations have resulted in harassment by digital vigilantes, people who take it upon themselves to degrade and punish supposed wrongdoers.

Privacy watchdogs contend that a major issue in the practice of gathering evidence via social media is reliability. Account identity theft on platforms like Facebook is rampant. Sophisticated **social engineering** tactics can damage a victim's reputation and get the individual into legal trouble while the victim is unaware of what's happening.

For example, a hacker can open an account under your name, borrowing some of your posted photos and posting personal details, leading others to believe the manipulator truly is you. If risqué, hateful, or embarrassing material begins to appear online, apparently authored by you, it can threaten your job, suggest you are a predator, link you to unsavory characters and causes, and ruin your personal relationships. Employers and friends may believe they've uncovered a hideous side of your personality, when in reality, the information is being generated maliciously by the "other you."

Surveillance critics worry that even information collected and stored by top-level government security agencies is at risk of being hacked. Agencies including the NSA, CIA, and FBI have given assurances that they maintain ironclad protection against cyber intrusion. As an example, at its website, the FBI's National Crime Information Center states, "NCIC policy establishes a number of security measures to ensure the privacy and integrity of the data. The information passing through the network is encrypted to prevent unauthorized access. Each user of the system is authenticated to ensure proper levels of access for every transaction. To further ascertain and verify the accuracy and integrity of the data, each agency must periodically validate its records. Agencies also must undergo periodic audits to ensure data quality and adherence to all security provisions."

Data hacks make sensational news, as illustrated by this headline in the *Guardian* in London in 2013.

Some skeptics are not convinced. They point to hacks of computers at the US State Department, White House, National Oceanic and Atmospheric Administration, and US Postal Service. They also cite local-level invasions such as the recent cyber ransoming of a police department in New Hampshire.

Privacy disputes have arisen between employees and their employers over mobile phone monitoring. A workplace trend that began around the turn of the century was dubbed "BYOD"—"bring your own device." A growing number of workers owned powerful smartphones and mobile computers—more powerful or easier to use than similar equipment their employers provided for them to use in their work. They wanted to be allowed to use their personal devices instead. Timidly, many companies relented. They drafted BYOD policies that stipulated which brands and models of personal devices could be used for work-related tasks, and for what specific purposes. Information security, obviously, was employers' great concern.

The question became how much, if any, oversight the employing firm should have over a worker's mobile device, whether it was issued by the company or belonged to the employee. Many workers assumed they were free to use the device however they wished, without asking permission or following a company policy. Some took the liberty to upgrade apps on company-related phones and even to let their children use them.

Large businesses, government agencies, hospitals, and other organizations have suffered cyberattacks as a result of employees' carelessness or wrongful use of company-connected smartphones and tablet computers. Hackers have been able to enter firms' computer networks and databases via an employee's mobile equipment. For that reason, many corporate IT (information technology) departments insist on the right to monitor mobile devices that have connections to the company's information network. In some situations, employees protest that even though the company issued their phones, it was done so with the understanding that the workers could use the phones for personal as well as business purposes; thus, monitoring by the IT staff constitutes at least a partial invasion of privacy.

Complaints Against Agencies

Leading security and law enforcement agencies have borne the brunt of protests and legal proceedings initiated by civil libertarians and watchdog groups. However, surveillance technology at all levels often comes under scrutiny.

Data Held Hostage

Of all the things that can go wrong with collected surveillance information, one of the most sinister is having it be used to the detriment of the entity that collected it. Cyber extortion is the virtual commandeering of computer systems and/or data by hackers, with a demand for ransom in order to retrieve it.

A form of malware called ransomware has become pervasive on the internet. Invading network servers and personal computers, it locks access to files by cyber-encrypting them. For a fee, to be paid in **Bitcoins** so it can't be traced, the computer owner can receive a cyber key to unlock the files.

Particularly chilling examples of cyber blackmail are when medical facilities are targeted. A California health-care center in 2016 paid some $17,000 in Bitcoins to regain access to its computer system. Ransomware attacked the system when a hospital employee opened an attachment to an e-memo that appeared to be a financial statement. Hospital administrators decided paying the ransom was the best way to get their computers running again. A prolonged disruption would have meant patient data would be unavailable to doctors and various health services would have been suspended. In that kind of situation, lives theoretically could be at risk.

In an article for *Wired*, Kim Zetter observes, "Hospitals are the perfect mark for this kind of extortion because they provide critical care and rely on up-to-date information from patient records. Without quick access to drug histories, surgery directives and other information, patient care can get delayed or halted, which makes hospitals more likely to pay a ransom rather than risk delays that could result in death and lawsuits."

Other types of businesses especially enticing to cyber blackmailers are major law offices, which store confidential client information. Government offices likewise have been blackmailed.

The role of the National Security Administration and its operations has brought into focus the pros and cons of surveillance and the technologies different agencies employ. The NSA without question has prevented foreign actors from infiltrating the US government's information systems and obtaining material that might impair the country's position in military and economic negotiations. In doing its work, it also has been accused by American privacy groups of invasive practices. The NSA has been accused of spying on the United States' own citizens, sometimes with questionable justification.

A storm of international controversy swirled around the agency in 2013 after Edward Snowden, an employee of a National Security Agency contracting company, leaked classified information about certain activities of the NSA and its surveillance partners in other countries. Those revelations and the aftereffects are explored in depth in a companion volume in this series, *Edward Snowden: Heroic Whistleblower or Traitorous Spy?*

Many citizens don't notice cameras installed in public places, such as this unit in a grocery store.

From the National Security Agency's inception, its operations have been viewed suspiciously by some legislators. Information the NSA supplied to the US military was critical to the nation's strategies and operations during the Korean War and the Vietnam War. But a 1975 US Senate investigation revealed that the NSA also had been examining telegrams and other correspondence of civilians, notably leaders of the 1960s civil rights movement and political dissidents. This resulted in the 1978 Foreign Intelligence Surveillance Act, which set what types of data the NSA was authorized to obtain.

After the terrorist attacks of September 11, 2001, the NSA was given new powers. For example, it was allowed to examine emails and listen in on phone calls of countless American as well as foreign persons of interest, without a court-issued warrant. Legal and political privacy advocates protested. President George W. Bush in 2007 terminated the policy of NSA wiretaps without warrants. The Snowden leaks in 2013 resulted in further restrictions on the agency.

Privacy watchdog groups also have questioned Central Intelligence Agency surveillance practices for many years. In the FAQs page at its website, the agency states: "By law, the CIA is specifically prohibited from collecting foreign intelligence concerning the domestic activities of US citizens. Its mission is to collect information related to foreign intelligence and foreign counterintelligence. By direction of the president in Executive Order 12333 of 1981 and in accordance with procedures approved by the Attorney General, the CIA is restricted in the collection of intelligence information directed against US citizens. Collection is allowed only for an authorized intelligence purpose; for example, if there is a reason to believe that an individual is involved in espionage or international terrorist activities."

Doubters suspect CIA agents at times exceed their authority and misuse surveillance technology. They harbor similar suspicions of the Federal Bureau of Investigation, US Border Patrol, and other federal agencies. Suspicions filter down to state law enforcement agencies, local police departments, and private investigation firms.

Civil libertarians are particularly critical of closed-circuit TV (CCTV) monitoring. Local governments and private businesses and citizens have CCTV devices placed in millions of locations throughout multiple countries. They record goings-on in public buildings and parks, airports, train and bus stations, schools, hospitals, libraries, shopping malls, and streets, as well as inside police facilities and prisons. This technology has become accepted by the majority of people in most nations because it has led to the capture of suspects in sensational crimes worldwide.

One of the most famous instances came after the horrific bombing at the Boston Marathon in April 2013. Law enforcement officials collected surveillance video from the approximately two hundred businesses near where the bombs went off, and they used that video footage to help in identifying two suspects in the bombing. Some governments, though, do not allow CCTV cameras to be installed in public places, holding that they intrude on civil liberties.

Privacy Watchdog Organizations

Watchdog groups generally are nonprofit organizations that rely on funding by the public. Their staffers monitor news reports and citizen complaints about surveillance issues and research details and effects of government projects. Privacy advocates are active internationally and in communities. Well-known organizations include the following.

American Civil Liberties Union

The American Civil Liberties Union's (ACLU) stated mission is "to defend and preserve the individual rights and liberties guaranteed by the Constitution and laws of the United States." ACLU lawyers frequently represent people and causes they believe are treated illegally or unfairly, including civil dissidents, immigrants, prisoners, and members of special interest minority groups. The union claims it "takes up the toughest civil liberties cases and issues to defend all people from government abuse and overreach."

With the explosion of internet-related activities and habits since the beginning of the century, the use of the internet for police surveillance has become one of the organization's focal subjects. As an example, in a website post titled "Social Media Helps Police Spy on Activists," the group asserts that "police are using social media surveillance companies' analytics and search capabilities to monitor activists protesting police brutality." The report states, "Social media is a driver for activism, political conversation, and the fight for human rights. We need to make sure it continues to be a safe forum for millions to connect about the most important issues in our lives—and can't be used as funnels for a surveillance database."

The ACLU points out that its members do not necessarily agree with all of the individuals and groups the union defends. However, it is committed to "defend their right to free expression and free assembly."

Electronic Frontier Foundation

The Electronic Frontier Foundation (EFF) defines itself as "the leading nonprofit organization defending civil liberties in the digital world." It was established in 1990, when the internet as we know it was in its infancy. According to its statement of purpose, the foundation "champions user privacy, free expression, and innovation through impact litigation, policy analysis, grassroots activism, and technology development. We work to ensure that rights and freedoms are enhanced and protected as our use of technology grows."

The EFF staff includes cutting-edge technologists, activists, and lawyers. They work to "defend free speech online, fight illegal surveillance, advocate for users and innovators, and support freedom-enhancing technologies." While they investigate and report on flaws and abuses with surveillance technology, they also explain how law enforcers and other legitimate surveillance professionals can use technology more effectively and ethically.

For example, in a September 2016 report titled "Unreliable Informants: IP Addresses, Digital Tips and Police Raids," EFF technologists cite examples of investigations of innocent citizens as a consequence of misunderstanding the nature of IP address designations. A computer's location on the internet or another network is identified numerically by its internet protocol (IP) address. "Law enforcement too often overstates the reliability of IP address information in seeking warrants and other process (such as **subpoenas**), using metaphors that create a sense of certainty where it does not always exist," they write. "Additionally, courts often don't know what questions to ask about IP address information or how to evaluate its reliability."

The EFF acknowledges that IP addresses can be useful in finding the locations of criminal suspects "when combined with other information, such as ISP records." Otherwise, they assert, raids and investigations based on IP address data can be frightening and dangerous. They also can waste officers' time and resources, using search and arrest warrants that are issued improperly.

Electronic Privacy Information Center

The Electronic Privacy Information Center (EPIC), according to its statement of purpose, is a public information research center established "to focus public attention on emerging privacy and civil liberties issues and to protect privacy, freedom of expression, and democratic values in the information age." It focuses on law, public policy, and technology.

In December 2016, EPIC and other privacy groups filed a complaint with the Federal Trade Commission claiming

A monitor helps a mother check on her infant, but it can give others a look inside the home.

that certain robotic children's toys are, in effect, spying on children. Any toy that is connected to the internet could be suspect. "Talking companion" dolls can provide answers to children's questions in real time. Simultaneously, though, they record children's voices and transmit the voiceprints to a speech recognition company that, as it happens, is used by intelligence and military agencies. The toy manufacturer says the reason for recording the children is to improve their interactive experience with the toy.

Jeff John Roberts, writing in *Fortune* magazine, explains that the controversy heightens parental worries about "the privacy perils of a world where toys can be connected to the internet, and where a child may confide private secrets to a doll that records what they say. Even if a toy company has no intention to violate the child's privacy, the internet connection can still serve as a tempting target for hackers or ambitious marketers."

Among other initiatives, EPIC has urged the Federal Aviation Administration to take measures to ensure citizens' privacy from drone snooping. The FAA has maintained that its focus of responsibility is air safety, not privacy.

Privacy and Civil Liberties Oversight Board

The federal government itself has set up a privacy watchdog office. The Privacy and Civil Liberties Oversight Board (PCLOB) was established in 2007 as an independent, **nonpartisan** agency of the executive branch of the US government. The agency is part of the ongoing governmental response to terrorism in the aftermath of the September 11, 2001, attacks—in this case, to ensure privacy while combatting terrorists. "The PCLOB's mission is to ensure that the federal government's efforts to prevent terrorism are balanced with the need to protect privacy and civil liberties," the agency states at its website.

The board provides oversight and advice about the president's policies, procedures, regulations, and shared information that pertain to protecting Americans. It has the authority to review executive actions intended to protect the nation from terrorism "in order to determine whether such actions appropriately protect privacy and civil liberties and whether they are consistent with governing laws, regulations, and policies regarding privacy and civil liberties." The board has access to executive agency records, including classified documents. It is empowered to "interview, take statements from, or take public testimony from any executive branch officer or employee."

Freedom of Information

A key tool used by watchdog groups in monitoring government surveillance practices is the federal Freedom of Information Act (FOIA). The FOIA, which became effective in 1967, gives citizens the right to request access to federal agency records. It has been updated to require federal agencies to publish on the internet, without being asked, frequently requested documents and certain other categories of records.

Congressional representatives and journalists during the late 1950s and 1960s mounted a persuasive campaign, arguing that the public is entitled to be informed about the activities of its government, some of which are politically sensitive. Since the law was passed, numerous organizations and individuals have filed FOIA requests and lawsuits against various government entities, seeking to bring to light details about controversial activities. The original act has been amended and strengthened, and states have adopted their own free information acts.

By law, agencies must provide requested information unless they can argue successfully why it should be kept secret. Several possible exemptions frequently are argued. For example, intelligence agencies must not disclose classified information. They cannot release classified information requested by foreign governments or their representatives.

Another important law is the Privacy Act of 1974. It regulates the personal information that federal agencies can collect and distribute about individuals.

Many consumer drones are equipped with powerful video cameras. Only the operator knows what's being videoed.

Debate Continues

A drone flying over a residential neighborhood in Kentucky in July 2015 was shot down with a shotgun. The citizen who downed the drone said his daughters, who had been sunbathing in their fenced backyard, came in and told him a drone was flying over their home and those of neighbors. When he went to look, he said the drone was flying around a neighbor's yard. He got his shotgun and determined to shoot the craft if it came over his own house, which it did.

Afterward, the owner of the drone contended he had been asked to fly it over a friend's house nearby. He claimed he was not spying on anyone and the drone never hovered near the ground.

Interviewed by WAVE 3 News in Louisville, Kentucky, the shooter stated, "We live in a society now where we don't know what these people are doing. We don't know if they are pedophiles looking for kids, we don't know if they are thieves, we don't know if it is ISIS."

Regardless, the shooter was arrested for wanton endangerment and criminal mischief. At trial three months later, however, a county judge agreed with the defendant that the drone maneuvers represented a privacy invasion and that he "had the right to shoot this drone." She cited the testimony of two witnesses who said the drone was flying below the tree line, proof that privacy was being invaded, and dismissed the case.

It was not the only incident of citizens shooting down drones in recent years. Going forward, the case raises complex legal questions. Basically, the wary resident believed he had a right to protect his privacy. The drone pilot's lawyer and other drone enthusiasts contended that the federal government alone has authority over airspace, and that therefore it's illegal for a citizen to shoot down any aircraft.

Law enforcement authorities generally take a traditional stance: if you feel threatened, unless it's a life-or-death emergency, don't attempt to resolve the problem yourself; call the police. However, drone takedowns suggest that the spiraling debate over surveillance technologies has entered local landscapes and airspaces. In the neighborhood realm, some citizens feel emboldened to protect their privacy rights as they see fit. The situation has become not only legally challenging but potentially dangerous.

Issues involving privacy rights have become confused, especially with the plethora of citizen-operated drones. In the drone-shooting incident described above, many people agree with the judge that the man was within his rights to shoot down an aircraft he believed was intruding over his property and that of his neighbors. The owner of the drone and legions of other drone hobbyists and business pilots protested. They say antagonists should be held liable for damage to a downed craft and for any damage or personal injury that might be caused if a UAV crashes or zooms out of control.

Analysts of legal and judicial issues wonder when, or if, it will be possible to effectively enforce drone regulations and laws. For example, how can authorities know when a so-called recreational drone pilot crosses the line and uses the craft for pay, perhaps being engaged by a real estate company to take aerial photographs of houses on the market? Some commercial drone operators may be ignoring commercial certification requirements. Proving a drone is being used illegally or immorally is very difficult if not impossible.

The IoT: New Tech for a New Century

Another wide-open field of emerging, pervasive surveillance in this century is the so-called internet of things (IoT). With wireless technology, millions of personal and household devices today are connected to the internet. They range from smart watches to alarm clocks to automatic coffeemakers to home appliances to health and fitness monitors. They also include vehicle control systems. This technology remotely connects devices with their owners and with one another.

Consumer advocates and government officials are concerned that the IoT also opens wide new avenues for privacy invasion and cybercrime. For example, if a burglar gains electronic access to your household network of connected devices, this could reveal details about your daily routine. Also, people could be watching you. In a case in 2013, a Miss Teen contestant from California revealed someone had taken images of her through her laptop and said he would keep the photos out of the public realm for a fee. The alleged hacker was arrested. Meanwhile, product manufacturers could be mining information about customers' activities.

The internet of things can turn appliances such as "smart" coffeemakers into surveillance tools.

Protecting Sensitive Information

Privacy advocates for generations have decried the compiling of personal information about citizens. Whether data gathering routinely is conducted by police and other government agencies, businesses that keep customer account records, marketers, or other individuals, skeptics warn that it can lead to problems. Data collection is a form of surveillance, keeping track of a person's activities and interests. Even if information is collected for beneficial, constructive purposes, it can be stolen and used to wreak mayhem.

In the digital age, issues concerning data gathering via the internet and computers have multiplied. Security departments and contractors for businesses, financial institutions, and government agencies continually seek new ways to foil unwanted snooping and data theft. While security specialists strive to block spies and thieves from digital break-

Fast Fact

Fast Fact

Cisco Systems, Inc., predicts that the number of devices connected via the internet of things will increase from fifteen billion in 2016 to between fifty billion and two hundred billion in 2020. Some forecasting organizations estimate there will be even more.

ins, intelligence and law enforcement authorities track and apprehend miscreants. In recent years, they have pursued various strategies.

For government authorities and security firms, thwarting digital surveillance and data theft by criminals is only one of the challenges. Another is determining who is behind threatening and damaging activity. "Finding irrefutable evidence that links an attacker to an attack is virtually unattainable, so everything boils down to assumptions and judgments," states Mark McArdle, chief technology officer at the eSentire cyber security company, in a press release dated September 30, 2016.

Log data and other archived network and server information can provide clues as to which malware program was used and possible suspects. However, McArdle points out that the major players in cybercrime are extremely sophisticated. It isn't unknown for them to intentionally leave behind "breadcrumbs" of trace evidence meant to steer investigators in the wrong direction.

Shifts in Public Opinion

Public and legislative sentiment supporting widespread surveillance measures peaked in the immediate aftermath of the September 2001 terrorist attacks, which were followed by anonymous **anthrax** mailings. Congress quickly passed the USA PATRIOT Act. A large portion of the lengthy legislation allowed for heightened intelligence assets and enhanced surveillance powers in order for agencies to secure the country against terrorism.

From the outset, civil libertarians voiced alarm. Particularly troubling to them was the authorization of roving wiretaps on multiple telephones and the mass collection of phone records by the National Security Agency. The ACLU and other groups contended that the act facilitated spying on innocent Americans via phone, email, internet, bank account, and credit monitoring. Within a few years, the PATRIOT Act was revised, and specific privacy safeguards were put in place.

There always will be tension between positive and negative perceptions of gathering, storing, and distributing surveillance information. Even the ubiquitous, constantly used 911 call center is suspect in the minds of some. The 911 emergency reporting system in the United States and similar systems elsewhere are part of coordinated surveillance systems known as computer-assisted dispatch (CAD) technology. They gather information not just on the reported incident but also on the caller (who often is the victim of an accident, medical crisis, or crime). The name and address of the owner of the phone automatically are collected. This information provides a record of each time a call has been made from the phone to emergency services, and how every incident was resolved.

While it is difficult to deny the usefulness of this sort of information to emergency responders, there are those who are

Smoke billows from a doomed World Trade Center building following the 9/11 attacks.

wary of such automatic assimilation of data. Is the information absolutely secure? Will it be hacked? Will it be misused by people who have authorized access to it?

Oddly, while most Americans are at least somewhat concerned about over-surveillance in the modern age, millions seem lackadaisical in taking personal precautions. The use of social media platforms by billions of people around the globe places terabytes of new information about people online every minute of every day. Many social media users seem unaware that the details they reveal about themselves and the comments and images they post may be picked up by unfriendly virtual spies.

Surveillance by "Citizen Journalists"

An interesting twist in surveillance technology debates is the recording by bystanders of law enforcement activities. One of the issues raised is the justification of police use of force in certain instances. Bystanders' mobile phone videos have recorded police officers shooting and arresting suspects, sometimes in what seem to be disturbingly unwarranted circumstances.

The Electronic Frontier Foundation considers those bystanders to be "citizen journalists" who "have a free speech right to record and share videos of public police activity," according to an article posted at the EFF website in October 2016. The article states that "bystander recordings of police shootings have shined a much-needed light on law enforcement activities—greatly contributing to public discussion about police use of force."

The proliferation of citizen journalists in the internet age, when an at-the-scene video can be posted online instantly and go viral within minutes, has changed the way news is reported. In a 2015 *Digital Trends* article, author Keith Nelson Jr. surmises, "Simple math. There are more civilians than journalists. More civilian journalists mean more eyes searching for a story."

Skeptics caution that the few seconds of video captured by a bystander do not tell the whole story of what is happening and may be woefully misleading in terms of cause and result. They also note that a "breaking news" event can be prearranged

The use of smartphones for impromptu videoing and photography in public is common.

for sociopolitical purposes, with the citizen journalist poised to begin videoing at just the right moment. Citizen journalists typically have no training in the legal and ethical standards that are fundamental in professional journalism.

New Tech, New Questions

The debate surrounding surveillance technologies and practices is intensifying and becoming more complex as the century progresses. Tension between citizens' right to know and their right to privacy is nothing new, but it is taking new turns. At the heart of the controversy is how the technology is being used or, in the minds of some, misused.

Opponents of excessive surveillance typically refer to it as the "Big Brother" mind-set. "Big Brother" is the fictitious leader of an authoritarian society in *Nineteen Eighty-Four*, a novel by George Orwell that was published in 1949. In the novel, citizens are kept submissive by large posters that remind, "Big Brother Is Watching You." The character generally is considered to have been based on Joseph Stalin, the brutal dictator of the Soviet Union from 1929 until his death in 1953.

Privacy advocates often dub government surveillance agencies collectively as "Big Brother." They warn that the growing mass of information collected by the government about everyone in the country threatens freedom and individuality. Their wariness of personal data gathering extends to private corporations and marketers, health-care providers, academic institutions, and employers.

On the flip side, national and local police and security officials say surveillance is vital to the tasks they're assigned to perform. They also point out problems with watchdog groups and citizens surveilling the activities they conduct in the line of duty. For example, a bystander's video of an altercation or arrest can be posted immediately on the internet, where it may go viral quickly. Even if it shows no unwarranted use of force by police, its publication can impair proper prosecution of the case and undermine the judicial system. On a larger scale, agencies including the NSA, CIA, and FBI insist that their very effectiveness depends on their ability to conduct much of their work in secret. Exposure of details pertaining to certain investigations ultimately can harm the society they must protect.

Citizens are particularly quick to criticize modern surveillance technology and practices when they themselves are ticketed for a traffic violation or detected in a negative situation. Speeders scoff at speed control officers "hiding in the bushes" with electronic devices. Promiscuous spouses rant against private investigators who "pry" into their personal affairs.

The slogan "Big Brother Is Watching You,"
inspired by the novel *Nineteen Eighty-Four*,
became a battle cry of early privacy advocates.

In some cases, their arguments are difficult to dispute. Surveillance operations can backfire. Equipment may be flawed. The wrong people might find themselves under watch. Police may forcefully enter the wrong house and arrest the wrong people.

Still, many security professionals advise that, like it or not, people in the twenty-first century effectively are living with "zero privacy." Basic information about practically every individual in America and most foreign countries is easily available through simple internet searches. This includes birthdates, hometowns, educational and employment information, family relationships, phone numbers, residential addresses, and email addresses. Beyond that, experts say, you should not be surprised to discover that once-confidential data such as your social security number, driver's license number, mother's maiden name, and health records are available somewhere online. Data breaches of banks, retailers, and even government agencies with which you've done business or communicated can result in the compromise of all sorts of personal details and financial records in your name.

And you are being watched, literally. When you enter any building or area where security cameras are installed, your movements may be videoed and kept on record for a period of time. Even when you are hiking in the wilderness, it's possible you are being observed unknowingly via aerial technology— perhaps a police or military airplane or helicopter, perhaps a drone operated by a hobbyist nearby.

A recent dump of CIA documents on WikiLeaks reportedly shows that the agency has software and techniques for accessing smartphones, computers, and even internet-connected TVs. This software can get to information before it is encrypted.

New incidents that raise concerns about surveillance and privacy occur almost daily. As surveillance technology steadily becomes more powerful and more pervasive, such questions are bound to proliferate.

1608 Hans Lippershey in Germany invents the first working telescope.

June 26, 1794 French military officers in a hydrogen balloon observe movements of Austrian army units during the Battle of Fleurus and drop intelligence messages to ground forces.

March 7, 1876 Alexander Graham Bell receives a patent for the telephone. Within twenty years, the first secret wiretaps are being conducted.

July 1881 Alexander Graham Bell invents the first metal detector. Beginning in the 1960s, industrial metal detectors will enter service to detect concealed weapons.

February 8, 1900 The first Brownie box camera is shipped for sale. George Eastman's inexpensive camera introduces the concept of taking random snapshot photographs.

1914–1918 World War I military aviators conduct aerial surveillance flights, sometimes taking photographs of enemy installations below.

July 29, 1955 The first U-2 spy plane is successfully tested for the US government. The aircraft, fitted with powerful cameras, flies at 70,000 feet (21,336 meters), well above the range of detection or interception by standard enemy defense systems.

1955 First flight of the MQM-57 Falconer reconnaissance drone. Reconnaissance drones will become common during the Vietnam War and proliferate during the Persian Gulf War, Iraq War, and continuing military operations in the Middle East and elsewhere around the world. They also will enter regular service by police departments and government agencies such as the Border Patrol.

February 28, 1959 The Central Intelligence Agency and US Air Force launch the first Corona reconnaissance satellite.

July 19, 1960 The United Kingdom reports using video camera surveillance for the first time to monitor crowds during a visit by the Thai royal family. Law enforcement agencies in the United States will begin using video surveillance in 1965. Four years later, the first home security system employing video technology will be patented.

December 1975 Eastman Kodak engineer Steve Sasson develops a prototype for the first digital camera. By the end of the twentieth century, digicams will be replacing film cameras for most photography. An important benefit is the ability to transmit digital images quickly via the internet.

September 1987 First public tests on speed cameras in the US begin in Paradise Valley, Arizona.

September 18, 1996 The first internet protocol (IP) surveillance camera is introduced.

May 1997 The first significant social media friend-making site, Six Degrees, is launched. By the end of the century, social media and blogs will allow individuals to post and share personal information that can be accessed by governments and others.

June 2000 Samsung releases the first cell phone with a camera. By 2010, nearly all smartphones are equipped with digital cameras. This feature enables anyone to photograph anyone else, openly or surreptitiously. Images almost immediately can be distributed to contacts online or posted to social media for global circulation.

September 11, 2001 Terrorist attacks on major US targets prompt passage of the USA PATRIOT Act, extending unprecedented surveillance and security powers to government authorities. The act is signed on October 26, 2001.

2003 Facial recognition video technology is used to help track missing children.

May 2014 The NSA completes construction of the Utah Data Center, a facility designed to collect and analyze the largest amount of data acquired through surveillance in the world.

anarchist A person who rebels against all authority and advocates overthrowing the established order.

anthrax An infectious disease, caused by a bacterium, that can cause fatal lesions in human lungs.

Bitcoin Crypto or digital currency used for secretive, party-to-party online purchases with no banks involved. This is one of many such currencies known as Altcoins.

camcorder A video camera that records sounds and images.

child custody Care and control of a minor awarded by a court to one of the parents, typically in divorces.

classified Information that is kept secret for national security reasons.

confederacies Leagues or alliances of states or sovereign nations.

cybercriminal A person who uses a computer to commit a crime.

decommission To remove from service, such as when a ship is retired and is no longer used by a branch of the military.

deep web An area of the World Wide Web not indexed by typical search engines.

dissident One who disagrees with and speaks out against the official policy of an established government, religion, or other institution.

espionage The act of spying, usually by governments to acquire political or military information.

flotilla A fleet of boats or ships.

hacker A person who uses a computer, often reached remotely, to gain unauthorized access to information.

mainframe computer A large, fast computer used to handle multiple tasks and/or to serve information and processes to a network of smaller computers.

nonpartisan Free from political party affiliation or bias.

pager A small device that vibrates, beeps, or flashes a light to alert the user to an incoming phone message.

parole Conditional early release from a prison term.

polar Having to do with the North and South Poles. A satellite that performs a polar orbit passes over the poles and does not have an east-west orbital path.

probation Period during which a convicted criminal is granted freedom under supervised conditions.

radar A way of measuring direction, distance, and speed using electromagnetic waves.

reconnaissance Early surveillance of a location or situation to obtain preliminary information.

revenue Taxes, fines, or other income generated by a government entity, or money taken in by a business.

sedition The act of opposing or inciting to oppose legal authority.

social engineering Using deceptive social/psychological tactics to manipulate people into divulging personal or confidential information.

stakeout A period of secret surveillance of a building or an area.

subpoena A court order requiring a witness to appear at a judicial proceeding.

supercomputer An exceptionally fast, high-capacity computer.

warrant An authoritative written order issued by a government or legal official that gives police the right to make a specific search or an arrest.

wiretapping Connecting to a phone line or other wired communication conduit for the purpose of eavesdropping.

Books

Gillis, Tom. *Securing the Borderless Network: Security for the Web 2.0 World.* Indianapolis, IN: Cisco Press, 2010.

H. W. Wilson Company. *US National Debate Topic 2015–2016: Surveillance.* The Reference Shelf. Amenia, NY: Grey House Publishing, 2015.

Springer, Paul J. *Cyber Warfare.* Contemporary World Issues: Science, Technology, and Medicine. Santa Barbara, CA: ABC-CLIO, 2015.

Sulick, Michael J. S*pying in America: Espionage From the Revolutionary War to the Dawn of the Cold War.* Washington, DC: Georgetown University Press, 2012.

Online Articles

Mackey, Aaron, et al. "Unreliable Informants: IP Addresses, Digital Tips and Police Raids." Electronic Frontier Foundation, September 22, 2016. https://www.eff.org/wp/unreliable-informants-ip-addresses-digital-tips-and-police-raids.

"Recording Police Is Protected by the First Amendment, EFF Tells Court." Electronic Frontier Foundation,

October 31, 2016. https://www.eff.org/press/
archives/201610.

"Social Media Helps Police Spy on Activists." American
Civil Liberties Union. Updated November 29,
2016. https://action.aclu.org/secure/social-media-
spying?ms=web_161021__privacyandtechnology_
socialspying.

"What Is FOIA?" US Department of Justice. https://
www.foia.gov.

Organizations

Bureau of Alcohol, Tobacco, Firearms and Explosives

https://www.atf.gov

This site describes what this organization does, provides
news and updates on the subjects the organization
investigates, gives updates on rules and laws that relate to
the organization, and allows citizens to provide tips on
potentially illegal activity.

Center for the Study of the Drone at Bard College

http://dronecenter.bard.edu

News, interviews, feature stories, and links to publications that
cover all things related to drones are accessible at this page.

Central Intelligence Agency

https://www.cia.gov

News, blogs, and other resources are curated at this official site of the Central Intelligence Agency.

Electronic Frontier Foundation

https://www.eff.org

An organization dedicated to defending the rights of citizens in the digital world provides links to news, white papers, and social events for people interested in fighting surveillance of citizens by the NSA.

Electronic Privacy Information Center

https://www.epic.org

Videos, books, news, and information of the latest work done by this watchdog group are easily accessible at this website.

Federal Bureau of Investigation

https://www.fbi.gov

Crime statistics, news, information on the country's most wanted criminals, and details about what the FBI does are located on the bureau's official website.

International Criminal Police Organization

https://www.interpol.int

The international organization that connects police and investigative departments from many countries outlines its programs and projects and provides news on the latest major crimes from around the world.

National Oceanic and Atmospheric Administration

http://www.noaa.gov

The department's official website provides a wealth of information on our natural world, including reports on things such as fisheries and global warming.

National Security Agency/Central Security Service

https://www.nsa.gov

The NSA outlines its activities and how it protects the country on this official website.

Privacy and Civil Liberties Oversight Board

https://www.pclob.gov

This government agency is "committed to the protection of civil liberties and privacy in the nation's efforts against terrorism." Resources, news, and contact information can be found at its website.

Transportation Security Administration

https://www.tsa.gov

Information on the workings of the TSA is available here for travelers and curious citizens.

US Customs and Border Protection

https://www.cbp.gov/border-security

This site run by the Department of Homeland Security provides the latest news on border security and provides information of use to international travelers.

Books

Aid, Matthew M. *The Secret Sentry: The Untold History of the National Security Agency.* New York: Bloomsbury Press, 2009.

Harmon, Daniel E. *Special Ops: Military Intelligence.* Inside Special Forces. New York: Rosen Publishing, 2015.

Melton, H. Keith. *Ultimate Spy: Inside the Secret World of Espionage.* New York: DK Publishing, 2015.

Ribacoff, Daniel. *I, Spy: How to Be Your Own Private Investigator.* New York: St. Martin's Press, 2016.

Stephens, Sheila L. *The Everything Private Investigation Book.* Avon, MA: Adams Media, 2008.

Online Articles

Bauer, Katie. "William H. Merideth: Kentucky Man Charged After Shooting Down Drone." WAVE 3 News, July 30, 2015. http://www.wptv.com/news/national/kentucky-man-charged-after-shooting-down-drone.

Cooper, Allen. "Top DNC Staffers Out Following Email Scandal." *USA Today*, August 2, 2016.

http://www.usatoday.com/story/news/politics/
onpolitics/2016/08/02/democratic-national-committee-
ceo-resigns-dacey/87960580.

Dunn, Jeff. "Here's How the Latest Massive Yahoo Hack
Compares to Other Famous Security Breaches." *Business
Insider*, December 16, 2016. http://www.businessinsider.
com/biggest-hacks-of-all-time-chart-2016-12.

Foster, Tom. "10 Ways Drones Are Changing Your
World." *Consumer Reports*, December 14, 2016. http://
www.consumerreports.org/robots-drones/10-ways-
drones-are-changing-the-world.

Haisler, Dustin. "Top Ten Mobile Trends for Law
Enforcement." *Government Technology*, December 19,
2014. http://www.govtech.com/public-safety/GT-Top-
10-Mobile-Trends-for-Law-Enforcement.html.

Heiligenstein, Michael X. "A Brief History of the
NSA: From 1917 to 2014." *Saturday Evening Post*,
April 17, 2014. http://www.saturdayeveningpost.
com/2014/04/17/culture/politics/a-brief-history-of-the-
nsa.html.

Jouvenal, Justin. "The New Way Police Are Surveilling
You: Calculating Your Threat 'Score.'" *Washington Post*,
January 10, 2016. https://www.washingtonpost.com/

local/public-safety/the-new-way-police-are-surveilling-you-calculating-your-threat-score/2016/01/10/ e42bccac-8e15-11e5-baf4-bdf37355da0c_story.html.

Limer, Eric. "People Just Keep Shooting Down Their Neighbors' Drones." *Popular Mechanics*, May 27, 2016. http://www.popularmechanics.com/flight/drones/ a21072/people-just-keep-shooting-down-drones.

Martinez, Natalia. "'Drone Slayer' Claims Victory in Court." WAVE 3 News. Updated December 10, 2015. http://www.wave3.com/story/30355558/drone-slayer-claims-victory-in-court.

"Myanmar Debris: 'Mystery Object Lands at Jade Mine.'" BBC News, November 11, 2016. http://www.bbc.com/ news/world-asia-37946718.

"Mystery Debris That Could Be from Chinese Satellite Hits Mine." Sky News, November 11, 2016. http:// news.sky.com/story/mystery-debris-that-could-be-from-chinese-satellite-hits-mine-10653312.

Nelson, Keith, Jr. "The Citizen Journalist: How Ordinary People Are Taking Control of the News." *Digital Trends*, June 19, 2015. http://www.digitaltrends.com/features/ the-citizen-journalist-how-ordinary-people-are-taking-control-of-the-news.

Roberts, Jeff John. "Privacy Groups Claim These Popular Dolls Spy on Kids." *Fortune*, December 8, 2016. http://fortune.com/2016/12/08/my-friend-cayla-doll.

"Russian Satellite Hit by 'Space Junk' from Destroyed Chinese Spacecraft." RT Television Network, March 9, 2013. https://www.rt.com/news/russian-satellite-collide-chinese-044.

Shacklett, Mary. "10 BYOD Concerns That Go Beyond Security Issues." TechRepublic, August 20, 2012. http://www.techrepublic.com/blog/10-things/10-byod-concerns-that-go-beyond-security-issues.

Shane, Scott, Matthew Rosenberg, and Andrew W. Lehren. "WikiLeaks Releases Trove of Alleged C.I.A. Hacking Documents." *New York Times*, March 7, 2017. https://www.nytimes.com/2017/03/07/world/europe/wikileaks-cia-hacking.html?_r=0.

"Space Junk 'One of Earth's Greatest Environmental Challenges.'" Sky News, November 18, 2016. http://news.sky.com/story/space-junk-one-of-earths-greatest-environmental-challenges-10662029.

Storm, Darlene. "List of Hacked Government Agencies Grows: State Department, White House, NOAA and USPS." *Computerworld*, November 17, 2014. http://

www.computerworld.com/article/2848779/list-of-hacked-government-agencies-grows-state-department-white-house-noaa-and-usps.html

Whetstone, Thomas, and Jean-Paul Brodeur. "Police." Encyclopedia Britannica/High. Accessed February 13, 2017. http://school.eb.com/levels/high/article/108569.

Zetter, Kim. "Why Hospitals Are the Perfect Targets for Ransomware." *Wired*, March 30, 2016. https://www.wired.com/2016/03/ransomware-why-hospitals-are-the-perfect-targets.

Daniel E. Harmon has written thousands of magazine and newspaper articles and more than one hundred books, mainly educational series volumes on a wide variety of topics. Related to this book are his works on military intelligence operations, the FBI, the ATF, cryptography, the US armed forces, global commerce, and careers in internet security and criminal justice. Harmon is the long-time editor of the *Lawyer's PC*, a legal technology newsletter; the newsletter regularly reports on cybersecurity incidents and statistics. A one-time security officer, Harmon is a drone hobbyist. He also enjoys writing historical crime fiction. He lives in Spartanburg, South Carolina.